THE
ROYAL YEAR

THE ROYAL YEAR

A YEAR IN THE LIFE OF THE ROYAL FAMILY

Edited by
Lynn Picknett & Shona Grimbly

ORBIS · LONDON

Printed in Italy
ISBN 0 85613 821 5

Contributors:
Sam Elder, Sarah Litvinoff, Nicolas
Locke, Jane Owen of *Sunday People*,
Paul Stelb and Sally Wood

Picture researchers:
Vivien Adelman and Fenella
Greenfield

Editorial assistants:
Vida Adamoli and Catherine Harding

Designed by Ray Kirkpatrick
and Anne Sharples

Picture acknowledgements
Reproduced by Gracious Permission of Her
Majesty the Queen: 104/105 (T); 104/105
(BL); 105 (BR); 111 (B); All-Sport: 68/69 (T);
69 (R); 90; Alpha: 10 (L); 62; 74 (L); 74/75; 75
(T); 75 (B); 112/113; 112 (T); 116 (BR); 119
(B); 120; 132; 133 (TR); 135 (B); 137; 137 (TL);
138 (BR); 141 (T); 141 (B); 145 (T); 146/147;
158 (T); BBC Enterprises: 122; 131 (B); 143
(TR); BBC Hulton Picture Library: 20/21 (B);
41 (TR); Brunswick Printing and Publishing
Co. Ltd: 118 (T); 118 (B); Camera Press: front
cover (TR, BR); back cover (BL); 21; 45; 58/
59 (BL); 59 (C); 78/79; 92/93; 125 (B); 127 (B);
142/143; 148; 156/157; Camera Press/Snow-
don: back cover (main picture); Lionel Cher-
ruault: 78; 81; 94 (TL); 94/95 (B); 95 (R); 96
(T); 96 (BL); 96/97 (B); 97 (T); 97 (BR); 117;
150; John Frost Newspapers: 39 (BR); Tim
Graham: back cover (CL, TC); 2/3; 8/9;
10/11; 12 (BL); 12/13; 13 (TR); 13 (BR); 14/
15; 16 (B); 18/19; 24 (C); 24 (R); 26; 26/27; 27

(TR); 27 (BR); 28/29; 32; 36 (BL); 36 (BR); 37
(BR); 46; 47 (T); 47 (B); 50/51 (B); 51 (T); 51
(BR); 54 (TL); 54 (TC); 54 (TR); 54/55 (B); 56/
57; 57 (T); 57 (B); 58/59 (TL); 59 (T); 59 (B);
60; 60 (L); 60 (C); 60 (R); 62/63 (T); 63; 66/67
(TL); 66 (BL); 66/67 (BL); 67 (B); 70/71; 72;
72/73 (T); 73 (TR); 72/73 (B); 80 (B); 82/83 (B);
84/85 (L); 85 (R); 88; 89 (TL); 89 (B); 89 (TR);
92 (B); 100 (B); 100/101 (C); 102 (B); 105; 108/
109 (TL); 109 (T); 108 (B); 109 (B); 112 (B);
113 (BL); 113 (TR); 114/115; 119 (T); 121 (T);
126/127 (T); 126/127 (B); 128; 129 (TL); 131
(T); 136; 149 (B); 153 (B); 154 (T); 154 (B);
154/155; 155 (BC); Brian Green: 67 (BR);
History of World War 2: 30/31 (T); 30/31
(B); Robert Hunt Library: 39 (R); 40 (BR);
Anwar Hussein: 86 (T); 86 (B); 86/87; 102 (T);
103 (TL); 103 (TR); 103 (B); 125 (T); 126 (T);
129 (B); 138 (T); 144; 146 (T); 149 (T); 155
(TR); Mansell Collection: 20/21 (T); Derry
Moore: 83 (T); 100/101 (T); 110 (B); The
News, Portsmouth: 42/43 (T); 42/43 (B);

Photographers International: front cover
(TL, BL, BC); back cover (TL); 1; 11 (R); 16
(T); 17; 19 (TR); 24 (L); 28; 33 (BR); 36/37 (T);
48/49; 77 (BR); 87 (T); 91 (T); 98/99; 99 (BR);
101 (B); 133 (TL); 133 (B); 138 (C); 145 (B);
158 (B); Press Association: 35 (B); 119 (C);
124 (B); 153 (T); Popperfoto: 40 (TL); 40 (BL);
40/41 (T); 41 (B); Rex Features: front cover
(C); back cover (TR); 4; 6; 12 (TL); 32/33 (T);
32/33 (BL); 34/35; 35 (T); 42 (L); 44/45 (T);
44/45 (B); 52/53 (T); 52 (B); 52/53 (B); 76/77
(TL); 76/77 (BL); 77 (TR); 82 (TL); 84; 91
(BL); 91 (BR); 93 (B); 106 (TL); 106 (BL); 106/
107; 107 (BR); 116/117 (T); 116 (BL); 121 (B);
130; 131 (C); 134; 135 (T); 140; 151; 152; 157
(T); 157 (BR); 157 (BL); John Shelley: 53 (T);
Spectrum Colour Library: 110/111; Frank
Spooner: 50 (TR); 64 (T); 64 (BL); 64/65 (B);
65 (T); Syndication International: 69 (L); 80
(T); 123 (T); 123 (B); 124 (T); 127 (T); 129
(TR); 139; 139 (BR); Topham: 22; 23 (T); 38
(T); 38 (B)

CONTENTS

Part I

A YEAR TO REMEMBER

The year 1984 was a memorable one for the British royal family. The Queen braved the threat of terrorist attacks to make a five-day State visit to Jordan and Prince Charles, in a lighter vein, braved bare-breasted grass-skirted beauties when he visited Papua New Guinea to open the new Parliament building. Princess Anne left the 'royal princess' image at home when she embarked on a gruelling tour of inspection of Save the Children Fund projects in Morocco, The Gambia and Upper Volta, pulling her weight as a member of the team and wearing practical safari clothes. And shortly before her 84th birthday, the Queen Mother made a three-day visit to the Channel Islands, in the course of which she demonstrated her remarkable skill at the pool table.

One of the high points of the year was undoubtedly the celebrations for the 40th anniversary of D-Day, when the Queen paid a flying visit to Normandy to commemorate, along with Britain's wartime Allies, the invasion of 6 June 1944 that marked the beginning of the end of the Second World War. With President Mitterrand of France the Queen visited the British war cemetery at Bayeux and then attended a ceremony at Utah Beach, where the American forces had landed. A very moving day ended at Arromanches, where the Queen took the salute at a marchpast of veterans of the campaign.

In February, two days after the Princess of Wales returned from her first official solo visit abroad – to Oslo – it was announced from Buckingham Palace that the Prince and Princess of Wales were expecting their second child. On 15 September Prince Henry, third in line to the throne, made his entry into the world at St Mary's, Paddington, and 22 hours later left with his parents for his home at Kensington Palace. A month or so previously his brother William had electrified the waiting world by uttering his first words into a microphone: 'Ant, ant. Daddy, look, ant!'

The year 1984 was also remarkable for the number of appearances that members of the royal family made on radio and television. Princess Margaret took part in an episode of BBC radio's *The Archers* and Princess Michael of Kent made an appearance in the television chat show *Private Lives*. Prince Andrew and Prince Edward appeared in a television film about their old school, Gordonstoun, and Prince Philip in a programme about his favourite sport, competition carriage driving. Prince Andrew also made two other appearances on television talking about his life as a naval officer, and Prince Edward was interviewed on Radio 1 about the undergraduate revue, *Glitterball Prizes*, which he produced at Cambridge. *Tomorrow's World* showed Prince Charles presenting awards and chatting to prize-winners. And on 26 September the children's television programme *Jackanory* featured Prince Charles reading his own story *The Old Man of Lochnagar* – it was no doubt keenly watched by Prince William. The year concluded, as usual, with the Queen's Christmas Day appearance in a film covering the highlights of the royal year.

PRINCESS IN WAITING

The slight signs of strain that the Princess of Wales had displayed on her solo trip to Norway were explained when on 14 February Buckingham Palace announced that she and Charles were expecting their second child. The statement created particular excitement because it was virtually unpredicted – one radio station, itching to break the news before the stipulated hour, played recorded baby cries all morning. The Queen and the Duke of Edinburgh were quoted as being 'absolutely delighted' and a nationwide guessing game began. In the welter of public speculation over the sex of the child and the most likely names, only three things could be safely assumed: that the new arrival would be third in line of succession; and that Diana would continue to have her own ideas on how to handle her pregnancy and exactly which engagements she would undertake leading up to the birth.

The Princess of Wales had firmly established her own style while carrying William. She had broken with the royal tradition of expectant mothers who had interpreted the idea of confinement literally by tucking themselves away behind palace walls and emerging only occasionally into the public eye. Throughout her second pregnancy Diana maintained a heavy schedule of appearances until well into her sixth month, at the same time consolidating her status as one of the most professional and diligent members of the royal family. Gone were any vestiges of shyness, and the efforts to ease pressure on the Princess seemed unnecessary as she worked the round of visits to hospitals, community centres and factories with a new-found aplomb.

Diana's determination to maintain control of the conditions surrounding her pregnancy showed in other ways. Throughout, she steadfastly refused to be told the sex of the baby that the scans at her regular medical check-ups could have easily ascertained. Additionally, to the consternation of royal gynaecologist George Pinker she said she wanted to have the baby at home rather than (as he insisted) at St Mary's, Paddington. Although her last official engagement was at the Odstock hospital, near Salisbury, at the end of June, Diana continued to make appearances up to and even after the royal exodus to Balmoral in August. Two of these provided evidence of the Princess's desire to keep in touch with her old life as Lady Diana Spencer. In July she fulfilled a long-standing promise when she attended the wedding of ex-flatmate Laura Greig. Diana made sure her friend was the star of the day by slipping into the Knightsbridge church just 30 seconds before the bride was due to arrive. A sadly contrasting occasion was the funeral of her beloved uncle, Lord Fermoy, late in August. Although eight months pregnant, Diana made a 1000-mile (1600-kilometre) round trip from Balmoral to pay tearful respects to her uncle who, after a long depression, had tragically committed suicide.

To the people of Britain, the Princess of Wales was a constant source of delight during 1984. At public engagements her pleasure at being an expectant mother was evident to all – on a tour of a factory soon after the announcement of her pregnancy she was complimented on her figure by one of the workers. 'Thank you,' she replied with a rueful smile. 'It won't be like that for long.'

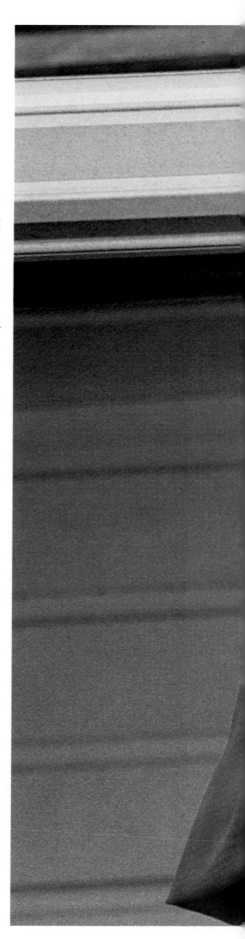

The Princess of Wales's determination that there should be as little fuss as possible over her condition showed in her choice of clothes, which demonstrated again that pregnancy need not mean frumpishness. Her positive approach was summed up by one of Diana's favourite designers, Gina Fratini, who said: 'The most wonderful thing about designing for the Princess of Wales is that she is so thrilled by pregnancy.' Fratini, together with Belville Sassoon and consultants from *Vogue*, developed a look – exploiting the current trend for voluminous garments – that managed to be both practical and fashionable. Camouflaging blacks and browns were banished, and the high yokes so often featured in maternity wear, which unflatteringly emphasise a growing bustline, were replaced by a series of stunning necklines.

Many of these incorporated eye-catching collars, with the sailor suit theme being seen in several outfits, such as the one that Diana, seven months pregnant, wore to watch Charles play during the International Polo Day at Windsor on 29 July – the couple's third wedding anniversary (previous page). Like a number of others, this outfit had first been seen in public before the birth of William, showing the Princess's new sense of economy. Evening wear for the expectant mother combined two distinct features: a low *décolletage* and a high waistline (centre, at the Royal Academy of Arts in May). Shortly after her pregnancy was announced, Diana began to wear the roomy but elegant coats she would wear throughout her months of waiting; she arrived in Birmingham for a charity pop concert (far left) in an elegant scarlet and black ensemble. Later the same evening Diana the trendsetter emerged when she met the band, Genesis, in a headline-making tuxedo trouser suit (left)

Diana delighted crowds everywhere with her informality (below, chatting to the public at Stoke-on-Trent) and always found time for a word with children (far right, at King's College Hospital). At the Albany Centre in Deptford Diana met another Princess (bottom left) with her father the Pearly King

Diana's maternity wardrobe included, as always, a range of hats made by milliner John Boyd (top left, a white straw hat worn at a factory opening in Wales). Many of her favourite Boyd creations are edged with a fine silk veiling (right, a dramatic black and white number and, overleaf, a blue pill-box for the Trooping the Colour procession)

IT'S A BOY!

His Royal Highness Prince Henry Charles Albert David, third in line to the throne, entered the world on the afternoon of 15 September 1984 in London. The official announcement was chained to the gates of Buckingham Palace at 5.55 p.m. and read: 'Her Royal Highness The Princess of Wales was safely delivered of a son at 4.20 p.m. today. Her Royal Highness and her child are both well.' In the streets outside St Mary's Hospital, Paddington, waiting crowds had learned of the birth half an hour before from a BBC technician who was relayed the news over his headphones and bellowed the message 'It's a boy!' A great cheer went up from the hundreds of wellwishers whose numbers had swelled throughout the day after Diana, accompanied by Prince Charles, arrived at the hospital at 7.30 a.m.

In mid-February newspapers had reported that Diana was expecting her second child. By all accounts the pregnancy was not an easy one although Diana, who was 23 in July, continued to perform official duties until ten weeks before the birth. From the outset she came under the care of Mr George Pinker, surgeon-gynaecologist to the Queen, and it was he who delivered the baby.

It was a damp, cold morning when Diana arrived at the hospital in the early stages of labour. She was escorted to a suite on the fourth floor of the Lindo wing and settled into the same room, overlooking Paddington Station, that she had occupied for Prince William's birth two years before. Prince Charles remained at his wife's bedside throughout the delivery of the new baby, who weighed in at a healthy 6 lb 14 oz (3.1 kilograms). First to be told the good news were the Queen and Prince Philip, who were telephoned at Balmoral; calls were also made to Diana's parents, Earl Spencer and Mrs Frances Shand Kydd. On leaving the hospital two hours later Charles walked into the glare of TV lights and rousing cheers from the crowds. He shook hands with wellwishers and quipped: 'We have nearly got a full polo team now.' His son, he said, had pale blue eyes and hair 'a sort of indeterminate colour'.

Next morning Charles was back at the hospital just after 9 a.m., this time with Prince William. Together they took the lift to the fourth floor, and as they emerged William saw his mother waiting for him outside the door of her room. With a shriek of delight he ran into her arms, and the family disappeared into Diana's room to inspect the new baby. For ten minutes the door remained closed, and hospital staff heard sounds of laughter and squeals of excitement. Then William emerged and left for home with his nanny, Barbara Barnes.

At 12.30 Prince Charles left for lunch, returning at 2.30 p.m. Then, five minutes later, the royal couple emerged together, Diana cradling the baby in a large white shawl. They paused briefly on the hospital steps before being whisked by car to Kensington Palace.

Having seen that everything was in hand at home, Charles drove out to Windsor to play in a specially organised polo match. Although his team was defeated, he had the satisfaction of scoring three of the four goals gained by his side. At the conclusion of the game the players opened a magnum of champagne and drank a toast in paper cups to Prince Harry and his parents. There – on Smith's Lawn, Windsor – it seemed an entirely appropriate manner of celebration.

Prince William met his baby brother for the first time on the morning after the birth. He arrived with his father at St Mary's Hospital (above), where he himself had been born, and spent a lively time laughing with his parents and holding the baby's hand before leaving for home with his nanny (below)

When she emerged from the hospital carrying Prince Henry enveloped in a shawl, Diana drew gasps of disbelief from members of the public. Just 22 hours after giving birth she was looking as ravishing as ever, wearing a cherry red crêpe coat over a striped silk dress, her hair a glorious flowing gold. One reporter was moved to write that when she left for home the Princess 'presented the picture of Ideal Motherhood'

Prince Charles and Diana pause for
photographers (opposite, inset) before
leaving for home with Prince Henry, not
yet 24 hours old. By then the baby's
names were known: Henry Charles
Albert David. Henry, of course, has
been the name of eight British Kings.
The last member of the royal family so
named was Henry, Duke of Gloucester,
who died in 1974. Charles derives both
from the baby's father and Diana's
brother, Viscount Althorp. Albert recalls
Queen Victoria's consort, and the baby's
great-grandfather who reigned as George
VI. David honours the Queen Mother's
brother, the late Sir David Bowes-Lyon.
A palace spokesman said that although
the baby would be christened Henry 'he
will be known as Harry.' And just 12
days after Prince Harry's birth, his father
reported that 'William says he is the best
thing since sliced bread'

BRINGING UP BABY THEN AND NOW

In the past it was assumed in the royal family that childrearing was solely the job of nannies. Even today, since royal mothers are working mothers, all of them have a nanny to share the work. But these days the children are not left solely in a nanny's care.

Diana would be horrified if William and Henry spent most of their time with Nanny Barnes, and were only presented to her washed and brushed at bedtime. Except when official duties call her away, she is fully involved with her children. She insisted on taking William on tour with her to Australia when he was only nine months old – something that would have been unthinkable in the old days. Princess Elizabeth of York (the Queen) was also nine months old when her parents departed on an extensive tour of New Zealand and Australia in January 1927. Her mother, who was quite 'broken up' at leaving the baby, returned a virtual stranger six months later.

When Prince Albert (George VI) was a baby he shared a nanny with his elder brother, Prince Edward (the Duke of Windsor). The nanny adored Edward, and wanted his love all to herself. She ignored and neglected Albert. The boys' parents, the Duke and Duchess of York, had no idea that the woman to whom they had entrusted their children was severely disturbed.

Prince Albert's nervous troubles probably started in the nursery. His nanny frightened him, and when he was old enough to learn to write he was made to use his right hand even though he was left-handed. It was hardly surprising that by the age of seven he had started to stutter.

Another problem for royal Princes of those days was that they were educated alone at home in their early and most impressionable years, and then suddenly thrust out, quite unprepared, into the challenging and alien environment of school or, perhaps, naval college. When Prince Albert was sent to Osborne naval college at the age of 14, he was a shy and highly strung boy with no defence against the bullying of the tough young naval cadets. They pricked him with pins to see if his blood was blue, beat him up, laughed at his stammer and called him 'Bat Lugs' because his ears stuck out.

His daughter, the Queen, was never sent to school and, apart from a few months with the ATS, she has never had a chance to live on equal terms with ordinary people. When she became a mother the Queen was determined that things would be different for Charles. He was sent first to a private day school in Knightsbridge, at the age of seven, and then, when he was nine, as a boarder to Cheam preparatory school in Hampshire. He was a desperately shy and unsure little boy, and when he went to Gordonstoun at 14 he found the rigours of life there so daunting that he telephoned his grandmother and begged her to intercede and have him taken away. However, he was eventually able to come to terms with school life, and from it gained confidence and an understanding of people outside his own royal circle.

The Princess of Wales has already made it clear that she wants William and Henry to be brought up as normally as possible, and their childhood promises to be happier than that of any royal children in the past.

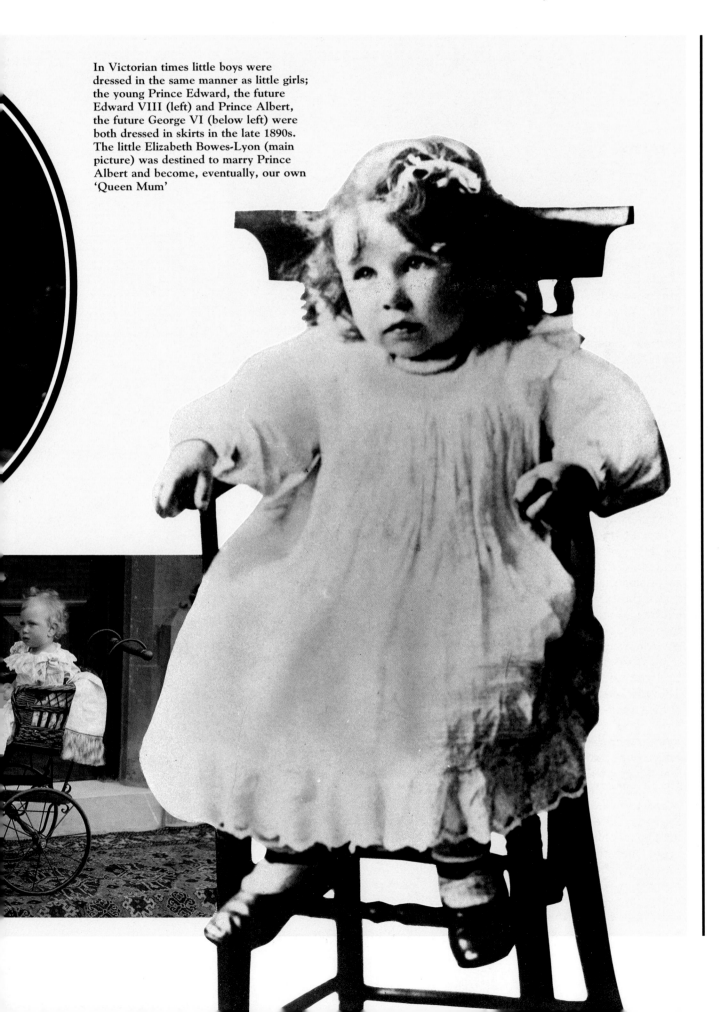

In Victorian times little boys were dressed in the same manner as little girls; the young Prince Edward, the future Edward VIII (left) and Prince Albert, the future George VI (below left) were both dressed in skirts in the late 1890s. The little Elizabeth Bowes-Lyon (main picture) was destined to marry Prince Albert and become, eventually, our own 'Queen Mum'

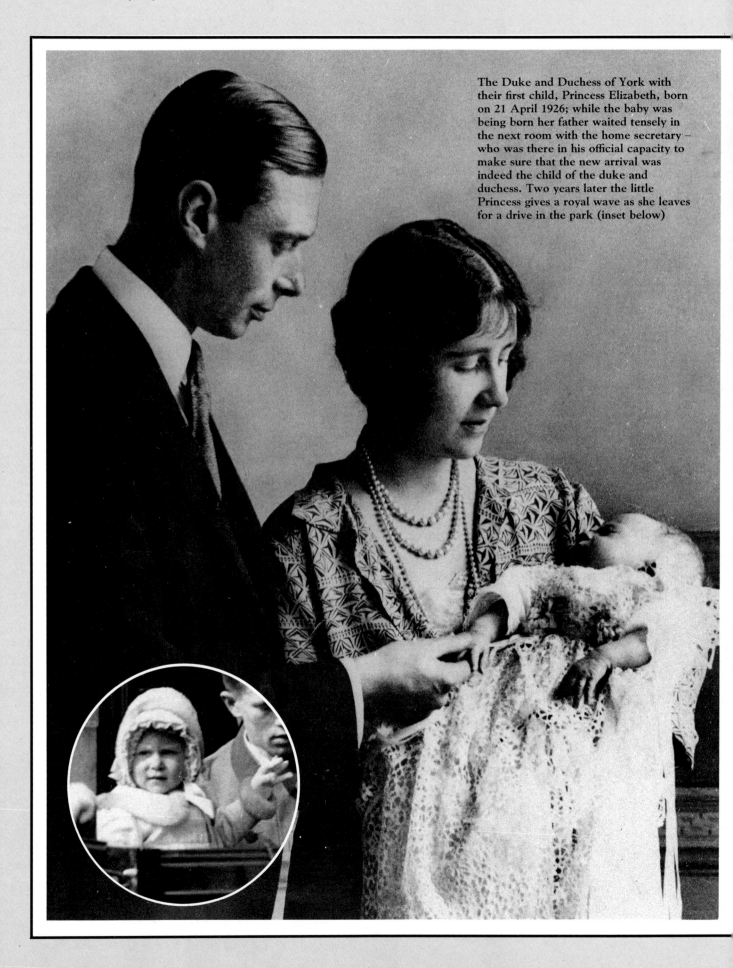

The Duke and Duchess of York with their first child, Princess Elizabeth, born on 21 April 1926; while the baby was being born her father waited tensely in the next room with the home secretary — who was there in his official capacity to make sure that the new arrival was indeed the child of the duke and duchess. Two years later the little Princess gives a royal wave as she leaves for a drive in the park (inset below)

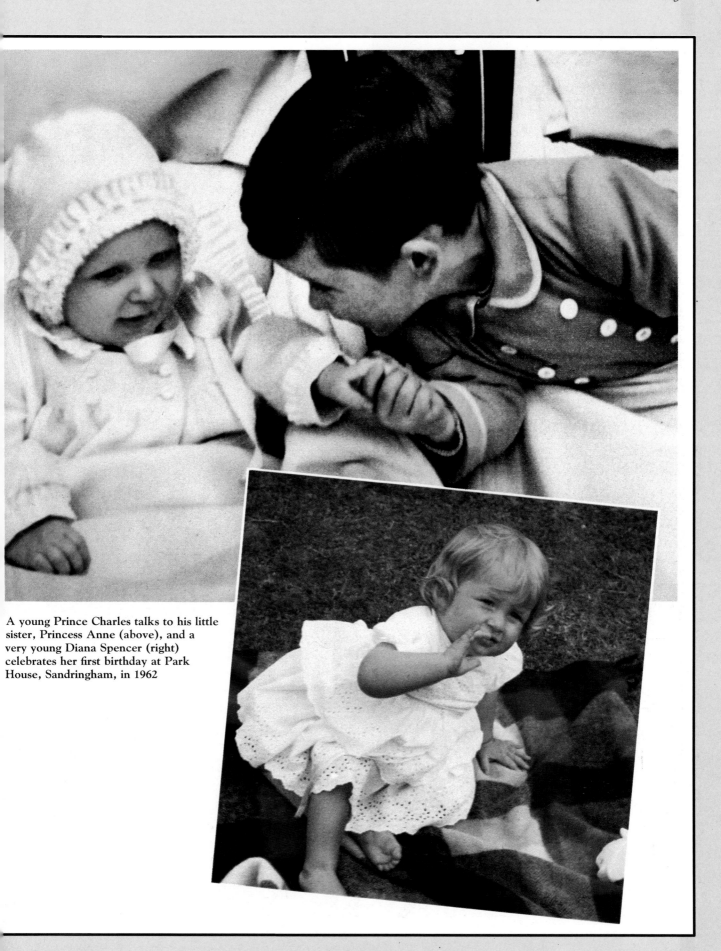

A young Prince Charles talks to his little sister, Princess Anne (above), and a very young Diana Spencer (right) celebrates her first birthday at Park House, Sandringham, in 1962

Pictures of Prince William taken on the occasion of his second birthday in the garden of Kensington Palace (this page and overleaf) show an inquisitive, cheerful little boy who would rather investigate the camera equipment than play with his ball

NOW WE ARE TWO

He doesn't know it yet, but while still a toddler Prince William of Wales has broken more rules than any Prince or Princess before him. His life so far has been an extraordinary mixture of royal precedents and normal upbringing. Despite his elevated background William's entry into the world on 21 June 1982 was at an 'ordinary' hospital, where Prince Charles was present during his wife's 16-hour labour and became the first heir to the throne to attend the birth of his child. Twenty-one hours later William recorded another 'first' when he appeared on the steps of St Mary's, Paddington, in Diana's arms – the earliest any direct heir to the throne had made his public début. He won't remember his maiden flight – a short hop to Balmoral – but the two-month-old broke a major royal rule. Second in line to the throne, he flew with his father – heir to the throne – thus jeopardising the immediate succession. Seven months later he travelled abroad to Australia – again unprecedented for one so young.

Charles and Diana's open enjoyment of William is an extension of their home life, and a part of their determination to bring him up as informally as possible. Even their choice of nanny is unconventional for royalty. Nanny Barnes – or 'Bar' as William calls her – has no formal training, does not wear the traditional uniform and, like all members of the royal staff, has been told that 'Wills' is never to be shouted at or smacked. It is Charles and Diana's belief that children need 'a lot of loving' and should be treated as individuals. The young Prince's penchant for breaking things and flushing his father's shoes down the toilet is happily endured as a natural phase, as is the curiosity that has led him to set off security systems at Balmoral and give his nanny and personal detectives the slip in St James's Park. Frequently exhausted by him, his mother has nicknamed William the 'mini tornado'.

Both his parents – whom William knows as 'Mummy' and 'Daddy', not 'Mama' and 'Papa' as is the royal rule – spend as much time with the Prince as they can. Nanny Barnes has to be prepared to hand over William for dressing, bathtime or any other impromptu visit. Whenever she is free to do so, Diana will sit down to lunch with William at his little nursery table, surrounded by toys, before going out for a walk together, or, if at Kensington Palace, a short pushchair ride round to see her sister, Lady Jane Fellowes. At night, Diana is known to curl up and sleep next to William's pine cot. The Prince and Princess of Wales also believe that constant stimulus is all-important for their son; he is spoken to as an adult, and his day and night nurseries at Highgrove are decorated with specially commissioned friezes of colourful cartoon animals. William is already an experienced swimmer and loves splashing about with his water-wings, with Charles close at hand, in the pools at both the royal homes.

Prince William's future will be increasingly spent in the public eye and his 'learning to be royal' lessons have started already. At the photocall for William's second birthday, Charles made a point of introducing his adventurous son to the television crews' microphones: 'Those big sausage-things record everything you say,' he warned. 'Start learning!'

Having mastered the art of walking (not to mention the royal wave) at 18 months, Prince William by the age of two had also learned to point at photographers and raise two fingers in a V-for-Victory salute. This last feat was captured on film after he successfully dragged his father down the steps of an Andover plane of the Queen's Flight at Aberdeen airport (below). Then it was off on holiday to Balmoral

D-DAY:
FORTY YEARS ON

On 5 June 1984 Prince Charles watched a drop by paratroopers of the 2nd Battalion, the Parachute Regiment (below), in the dropping zone in Normandy where, on the night of 5/6 June 1944, thousands of men descended to secure the eastern flank of the imminent invasion. The Queen (left) attended several ceremonies on 6 June to celebrate the 40th anniversary of D-Day, which started the liberation of western Europe.

Commemoration of the D-Day landings in Normandy was one of the most poignant events of the royal calendar in 1984. On 6 June the Queen and Prince Philip arrived in Normandy to attend a succession of services throughout the day to pay tribute to those who had taken part in the Allied invasion of German-occupied France 40 years before, an invasion that began the liberation of western Europe and was to lead to victory over Nazi Germany within a year. On the sands of the beach once code-named Utah, where men of the US VII Corps had clambered ashore in the gunmetal grey of a cloudy dawn, the Queen joined seven other Heads of State of Allied nations in the principal ceremony of the day.

Their arrival was preceded by a free-fall demonstration by paratroopers, including men from the Red Devils. President François Mitterrand of France, in charge of the day's proceedings, welcomed the other Heads of State: President Ronald Reagan of the United States, Pierre Trudeau of Canada, King Olaf of Norway, Queen Beatrix of the Netherlands, Grand Duke Jean of Luxembourg and King Baudouin of Belgium. As warships stood out to sea and fighters patrolled the skies, the dignitaries were given a 21-gun salute, watched a military parade and saw a flypast by Spitfires, Dakotas and a French aerobatic team. Flags were unfurled and national anthems played. In his address President Mitterrand paid tribute to the troops of D-Day. 'Let us salute those who have lived those hours and the veterans, particularly those here today, who are loyal and faithful to their youth,' he said. 'We owe them what we are today. Sometimes I wonder whether we have repaid them all we owe them.' Although no German representative had been invited, President Mitterrand spoke the language of reconciliation. The enemy, he said, had been the tyranny of Nazism, not the German people. 'So let us salute the German dead of this battle. Their sons demanded a new era.'

Pressure to open a second front in France had been exerted by Stalin from the time Germany invaded the USSR in June 1941. Not until early 1943, however, did the western Allies agree to launch an attack upon German-occupied Europe; they began to draw up plans for the assault, tentatively scheduled for 1 May 1944. 'This,' wrote Prime Minister Winston Churchill to President Roosevelt, 'is much the greatest thing we have ever attempted.'

General Dwight D. Eisenhower was appointed Supreme Allied Commander. Although he lacked battlefield experience he quickly showed himself to be a natural diplomat who won the respect of his subordinates for his skilful co-ordination of diverse talents and his ability to minimise national and inter-service rivalries. Command of the Allied land, air and naval forces was entrusted to three Britons: General Sir Bernard Montgomery, Air Chief Marshal Sir Trafford Leigh-Mallory and Admiral Sir Bertram Ramsay. Montgomery, a skilful tactician and superb motivator of men, expanded and refined the initial plan that called for an invasion of Hitler's Fortress Europe on the gently shelving beaches of Normandy rather than the nearer but more strongly defended Pas de Calais area.

By the spring of 1944 southern England had been transformed into one huge military camp. More than three million men were busy in reconnaissance, training and rehearsal; 1200 warships were being assembled, together with 4000 assault craft, 1600 merchantmen and 13,000 aircraft.

The date of 5 June for the invasion was abandoned because of gales, fog and high seas but Eisenhower took advantage of forecasts of slightly better weather and gave the go-ahead for 6 June.

In the invasion zone, German commander Field Marshal Erwin Rommel had greatly strengthened the Atlantic Wall by an impressive programme of fortification and the laying of six million mines, yet Germany's response to the threat of imminent invasion was one of indecision and delay. The German High Command, lacking advanced weather stations, was unaware of the improved weather that was forecast for the 6th and had stood down the coastal defences. Senior officers of the German Seventh Army were at a conference in Rennes, and Rommel himself was on leave, delivering a pair of fine handmade shoes to his wife for her birthday.

At 2115 hours on 5 June the BBC broadcast messages to France that included part of a verse by the poet Verlaine: '*Blessent mon cœur d'une langueur monotone*'. These words alerted the Resistance and other special agents to the imminence of the invasion and provided the signal to begin the disruption of road, rail and telephone communications. The Germans knew from the message that an invasion was on its way but they did not know for certain where it would land; the Pas de Calais was thought to be the most likely target, an opinion strengthened by Allied bombing of the area and other deception ploys. Rommel's long-held strategy was to halt the enemy on the beaches. He had remarked that 'the first 24 hours of the invasion will be decisive . . . for the Allies as well as Germany, it will be the longest day.'

Shortly after midnight on 5/6 June, British troops landed by glider and parachute around Ranville on the eastern flank of the invasion zone and seized the bridges over the Caen canal and the River Orne. Arriving in the area later in the morning Major-General Richard Gale, commander of the 6th Airborne Division, rode up to his staff and greeted them with a quotation from Shakespeare's *Henry V*: 'And gentlemen in England now a-bed shall think themselves accurs'd they were not here.'

By this time a perimeter had been established and the first French towns liberated. By then, too, paratroops of the US 101st and 82nd Airborne Divisions had descended – less accurately – on the western flank. A number of them were drowned in the swamps and flooded fields of the Cotentin Peninsula, and although Ste Mère Eglise was taken, other objectives remained unfulfilled at the end of that first day.

In the air, however, the Allies enjoyed total superiority; fewer than 100 fighters of the *Luftwaffe* took off on 6 June. Between midnight and dawn, 1000 RAF bombers unloaded 5000 tonnes of bombs on the German defences and they were followed by more than 1500 US bombers that struck along the coast and at roads and railways inland. As the assault troops went in they were supported by a sustained bombardment from 600 naval guns of the warships at sea.

On Utah, the most westerly of the five invasion beaches, units of the US VII Corps stormed ashore a few minutes after 0630 hours. They met only light enemy fire. Of the 23,000 men landed, just 12 were killed and 185 wounded. At Omaha, 10 miles (16 kilometres) to the east, the picture was bleak. The 34,000 men of 1st Infantry Division of V Corps were destined to launch a frontal assault against the most strongly defended beach of all. In a heavy swell 12 miles (19 kilometres) offshore, landing craft were swamped, many men were drowned, and more than 30 amphibious tanks, launched prematurely, sank in deep water 6000 yards (5400 metres) from the beach. On the beach itself the infantry met murderous fire from enemy emplacements. Furthermore, the American command had declined to use specialised armour that had been designed to neutralise minefields and clear paths rapidly through obstacles. So the beach became a bloodstained graveyard. It was left to small groups of men to attack with persistence and courage, and eventually breach the defences. With 1000 dead and 2000 wounded, Omaha exacted a heavy toll. On Gold, Juno and Sword, however, the British and Canadians were preceded by the specially equipped Sherman tanks that cleared a way through the minefields and, once the coastal defences were breached, armour and infantry could push inland.

Both Churchill and King George VI had been keen to watch the landings from sea, but George VI's private secretary managed to convince the King that the risks were too great. The King then sought to dissuade his prime

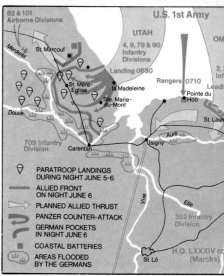

Four days after the initial assault went in, Churchill visited Normandy where he was briefed by Montgomery and Lieutenant-General Sir Miles Dempsey, who commanded the British and Canadians at Gold, Juno and Sword beaches (top). In the course of what he described as 'a long and very interesting day', Churchill inspected battle sites and presented decorations

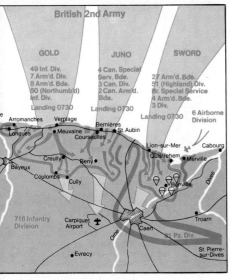

British 2nd Army

GOLD | JUNO | SWORD

49 Inf. Div.
7 Arm'd. Div.
8 Arm'd. Bde.
50 (Northumb'd)
Inf. Div.
Landing 0730

4 Can. Special
Serv. Bde.
3 Can. Div.
2 Can. Arm'd.
Bde.
Landing 0730

27 Arm'd. Bde.
51 (Highland) Div.
Br. Special Service
4 Arm'd. Bde.
3 Div.
Landing 0730

6 Airborne Division

Arromanches · Verplage · Bernières · St. Aubin
Longues · Meuvaine · Courseulles · Lion-sur-Mer · Cabourg
Creully · Beny · Quistreham · Merville
Bayeux · Coulombs · Cully · Ranville · Dives
716 Infantry Division · Carpiquet Airport · Caen · Troarn
Evrecy · Orne · 21 Pz. Div. · St. Pierre-sur-Dives

Although the landings of 6 June were immediately successful (above), few of the D-Day objectives on land were met. Bayeux was taken three days later but the Germans put up a fierce fight in Caen, which did not fall until mid-July and was reduced to rubble. In the west, the Americans did not succeed in liberating the port of Cherbourg until the end of June

minister from the enterprise; Churchill proved extremely stubborn. However when George VI pointed out that Churchill's death would be a shuddering blow to Allied morale, Churchill relented. Nevertheless he went to Normandy on 10 June, and the King went four days later.

The main anniversary celebrations in France fell on two days, 5 and 6 June. On the afternoon of Tuesday the 5th Prince Charles crossed the Channel to take part in ceremonies honouring the exploits of the paratroopers of the 6th Airborne Division who paved the way for the Allied landings. Wearing the uniform of colonel-in-chief of the Parachute Regiment, he arrived in a helicopter of the Queen's Flight in the original dropping zone at Ranville where British paratroopers had descended in strength. He watched a drop from two RAF Hercules of 68 paratroops of 2 Battalion, then drove by Land-Rover to the war cemetery, where 2500 soldiers are buried, and laid a wreath of red roses on the Cross of Sacrifice. A memorial service was followed by the Last Post and Reveille, and then a lament played by the man who had piped the British across Pegasus Bridge on the morning of D-Day itself. After unveiling a plaque dedicated to the memory of General Gale of 6th Airborne Division, Prince Charles extolled the division's 'great deeds of war'. He then shook hands with some of the 2000 veterans present before he left.

The following day at dawn the royal yacht *Britannia*, with the Queen and Prince Philip on board, nosed its way up the Caen canal past Pegasus Bridge, which was raised as if in ramrod salute. The skies were clear and the sun shining when the Queen, wearing a bright turquoise suit and matching hat, called upon the Mayor of Caen at the town hall at 11 a.m. To cries of '*Vive la Reine*' from crowds along the route the Queen then drove in a glass-topped Rolls-Royce to the church of St Étienne, where she saw the grave of William, Duke of Normandy (William the Conqueror).

The Queen returned to *Britannia* to host a lunch for visiting Heads of State before flying by helicopter to Bayeux and the largest cemetery of the Second World War in France. Wearing a peppermint green coat and a matching hat decorated with silk flowers and white net, the Queen was accompanied by Prince Philip to the cemetery where hundreds of British soldiers lie. She greeted President and Madame Mitterrand on their arrival and, after a band from the French Foreign Legion had given spirited renderings of the national anthem and the *Marseillaise*, the two couples walked together to lay wreaths at the base of the Cross of Sacrifice. The singing of the hymn 'O God our help in ages past' was followed by a prayer read by the chaplain-general of the British armed forces. As the strains of the Last Post faded, silence descended on the crowded lawns where some 3000 British veterans and their relatives had gathered in remembrance. After the Mitterrands had departed, the Queen and Prince Philip went on a walkabout, pausing to chat to old soldiers and war widows.

The Queen and Prince Philip were compelled by their schedule to fly by helicopter to the international ceremony at Utah beach, held just before 5 p.m., and then, 90 minutes later, to a short service at the Canadian cemetery at Beny-sur-Mer. When that had concluded they flew on to the final act of commemoration, held in the warmth of evening at Arromanches, north of Bayeux, shortly after 7 p.m. There the Queen and Prince Philip took the salute at a marchpast of 1500 British D-Day veterans, after which the Queen spoke in praise of the part played by the British armed forces and remembered those who had died in battle.

So ended a day of remembrance notable for the simplicity of the official services, which were transmitted around the world by television, radio and the Press. It was a time of thankfulness rather than joy. Not even the bustle of film crews, photographers and journalists could detract from the sombre nature of the ceremonies, which celebrated the crucial and crucifying 'longest day' that heralded the end of the Second World War.

Prince Charles, colonel-in-chief of the Parachute Regiment, flew to Ranville on 5 June to commemorate the part played by the 6th Airborne Division, who had parachuted in on the night before the troops went ashore at dawn on D-Day. At the war cemetery (far left) he thanked the veterans present for bringing peace to his generation and paid homage to members of the French Resistance who died fighting Nazism. The Prince unveiled a plaque (below left) to General Sir Richard Gale, commander of the 6th Airborne Division, who liberated Ranville on D-Day itself, and then laid a wreath on the Cross of Sacrifice (below) under the attentive gaze of old and young alike. The playing of the Last Post was followed by a lament on the bagpipes, after which the Prince chatted with some of the 2000 veterans who attended the service. Next day the Queen arrived in France on the royal yacht *Britannia* and first visited Caen. She called on the mayor and then, on a day celebrating the liberation of France from enemy occupation, she was, ironically, taken to the 11th-century church of St Étienne to view a plaque marking the tomb of William the Conqueror (left), who invaded England, defeated Harold and had himself crowned King of England on Christmas Day 1066

At Bayeux and Arromanches the Queen paid special tribute to British involvement in the Normandy landings. She laid a wreath with Prince Philip at the Bayeux war cemetery, as did President Mitterrand and his wife (left), and then mingled with the 3000 veterans, their families and war widows who crowded among the gravestones (top). In the early evening at Arromanches, the Queen and Prince Philip attended a marchpast by old soldiers (above). In her speech the Queen said: 'There are only a few occasions in history when the course of human destiny has depended on the events of a single day. June 6th 1944 was one of those critical moments.' She also quoted from Montgomery's eve of D-Day message to the men of the invasion force: 'To us is given the honour of striking a blow for freedom which will live in history; and in the better days that lie ahead men will speak with pride of our doings'

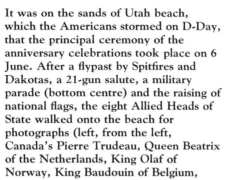

It was on the sands of Utah beach,
which the Americans stormed on D-Day,
that the principal ceremony of the
anniversary celebrations took place on 6
June. After a flypast by Spitfires and
Dakotas, a 21-gun salute, a military
parade (bottom centre) and the raising of
national flags, the eight Allied Heads of
State walked onto the beach for
photographs (left, from the left,
Canada's Pierre Trudeau, Queen Beatrix
of the Netherlands, King Olaf of
Norway, King Baudouin of Belgium,
President Mitterrand, the Queen, Grand
Duke Jean of Luxembourg and President
Reagan). The official party had watched
the earlier proceedings from a covered
dais (below). The day before at Ranville,
British and Canadian veterans had
participated in a ceremony (bottom far
left), attended by Prince Charles,
honouring the exploits of the 6th
Airborne Division, whose paratroopers
were the first Allies to land in Normandy
on D-Day and who liberated the first
villages and towns from Nazi occupation

FLASHBACK TO D-DAY

'Soldiers, sailors and airmen of the Allied Expeditionary Force: you are about to embark upon the great crusade, toward which we have striven these many months. The hopes and prayers of liberty-loving people everywhere march with you.' With these words the Supreme Allied Commander, General Dwight D. Eisenhower, began his Order of the Day for 6 June 1944. The Normandy invasion was the largest amphibious landing of all time. On D-Day alone over 150,000 men waded ashore on the five chosen beach-heads (left). Americans formed the single largest contingent, but the British (below) and Canadians also took part in strength along a stretch of coast 45 miles (72 kilometres) long from La Madeleine

to Ouistreham. General Sir Bernard Montgomery (above right, addressing Pressmen soon after the landings) exercised overall command of the initial assault. Stores and supplies followed the men and machines, and barrage balloons offered protection from attack (left). Allied losses were comparatively light: no more than 2500 men died on that one day although total casualties numbered 10,000. News of the success made compulsive reading (right), and soon Montgomery could report: 'a foothold has been gained on the continent of Europe'

The Daily Telegraph
and Morning Post

Printed in LONDON and MANCHESTER PRICE

No. 27,763   LONDON, WEDNESDAY, JUNE 7, 1944

ALLIED INVASION TROOPS SEVERAL MILES INTO

FIGHTING IN CAEN: 10,000 TONS OF BOMBS BLASTED WAY

PILOTS WATCH BATTLE, SAY "BEACHES OURS"

MASSED FIGHTERS HUNT IN VAIN FOR LUFTWAFFE

ALLIED ARMIES BEGAN THE LIBERATION OF EUROPE EARLY YESTERDAY MORNING WHEN THE GREATEST INVASION OF ALL TIME WAS LAUNCHED WITH LANDINGS FROM SEA AND AIR AT SEVERAL POINTS ON THE COAST OF NORMANDY. LATE LAST NIGHT FIGHTING WAS GOING ON IN THE STREETS OF CAEN, AN IMPORTANT ROAD JUNCTION 10 MILES INLAND AT THE BASE OF THE CHERBOURG PENINSULA.

Communiqué No. 2, issued from Gen. Eisenhower's H.Q. at midnight, stated that "reports of operations so far show that our forces succeeded in their initial landings. Fighting continues."

Pilots returning from the front last night reported Allied troops moving inland, with the "beaches completely in our hands." They said soldiers could be seen standing up on the beaches, where convoys were already assembling, while Allied tanks were moving towards Caen. Concentrations of German armour were seen moving towards the battlefield from the back areas.

Mr. Churchill made two statements yesterday. In his first House of Commons ... of the invasion ... been attained.

The map shows the area of the Allied invasion of Normandy. Fighting is raging inside Caen, and German reports last night stated that fresh landings were being made. All reports naming the landing areas are from German sources.

Midnight Communiqué
FIRST LANDINGS SUCCESSFUL

NAVAL CASUALTIES VERY LIGHT

Communiqué No. 1 from Supreme H.Q. Allied Expeditionary Forces, issued just after midnight, said:

Shortly before midnight on June 5, 1944 Allied night bombers opened the first great strength attack in very ...

The invading armies have successfully surmounted the first four or five hurdles of the operation, and it was felt at S.H.A.E.F. that there was definitely no cause for pessimism.

It was stressed, however, that it was too early yet to assess the position in Normandy, but opposition so far had been much less severe than expected, both on the actual sea passage and to the ... landing operations. The German ... not disclosed them-

"MANY DIFFICULTIES AND DANGERS BEHIND US"

Mr. CHURCHILL REPORTS INITIAL PROGRESS 'SATISFACTORY'

BY OUR OWN REPRESENTATIVE
WESTMINSTER, Tuesday.

Mr. Churchill, after giving an earlier communiqué ... in full on P3], in the House of ... the progress of the invasion, made ... business to-day

During the Second World War Buckingham Palace was bombed on several occasions; in four days in 1943 it was hit seven times. When the King and Queen inspected the badly damaged chapel with the prime minister, Winston Churchill, the resulting photograph (above) identified royalty with the sufferings of ordinary people. As the Queen remarked: 'Now I can look the East End in the face.' On a visit to France in late 1939 George VI inspected French troops (centre right) and in 1945, when she was 18, Princess Elizabeth joined the Auxiliary Territorial Service (right) as a driver and mechanic

The Queen's visit to Jordan went ahead despite the unrest in the country – and included some glittering occasions for the Queen (right). In a busy year, Princess Anne made a trip to the Olympic Games at Los Angeles (below, in rare moment to herself)

that began when the Princess visited Oslo, in Norway, for the première of the London City Ballet's *Carmen*. It was Prince Charles's turn to tour without his partner next, travelling to represent the Queen at the Independence Day celebrations in Brunei – a tiny but fabulously rich State on the island of Borneo. Seven days of festivities, at vast expense, climaxed in the Independence Day banquet, attended by 3000 guests – a magnificent affair, held in the Sultan's new £300 million palace.

In August Prince Charles jetted out to Papua New Guinea to open the island's new Parliament House. This was a relatively simple tour with low-key security, only a handful of Press and plenty of painted, chanting South Pacific islanders who presented 'Nambawan pikinini bilong Missis Kwin' with a club and some necklaces. At home, the year's major visits were those of the Emir of Bahrain, who stayed at Windsor in April, and the President of France, who made his State visit in late October.

DIANA IN NORWAY

The Princess of Wales's arrival at Oslo's Fornebu airport marked the beginning of her first official solo tour abroad. There to greet her, as representatives of King Olaf, were Crown Prince Harald and his wife Princess Sonja who acted as hosts for the 20-hour visit to Norway's capital. The Princess, crisply dressed in a three-quarter-length, cobalt blue suit, and hatless despite the sub-zero temperature, looked a little ill at ease without Charles but quickly got into her stride. She delighted the crowd – who had waited patiently in the ankle-deep snow just for a glimpse of her – by stopping to chat informally and, inevitably, to receive posies and gifts from awe-struck children.

That evening, Diana's visit with her hosts to the City Concert Hall was the highlight of Oslo's social calendar. The city dignitaries and those lucky enough to have tickets gathered in the foyer of the Concert Hall to await the arrival of arguably the world's most photographed woman, agog to see her for themselves. They were not disappointed. The Princess of Wales stepped out of her car into the sudden glare of popping flashguns wearing a full-length blue velvet cape – an elegant but sensible choice for the Norwegian climate. Once in the warmth of the building the Princess removed her cloak to reveal a stunning blood-red evening dress made of duchess silk and finely dusted with shimmering sequins.

After the performance of *Carmen*, a ballet based on Bizet's opera, the Princess went backstage to be introduced to the members of the London City Ballet troupe. Then she went on to the British Embassy for a dinner of smorgasbord – a Scandinavian speciality – and champagne. Her final engagement was the following morning, when she planted a fir sapling in the Embassy gardens.

Although the brief tour was considered a success – and certainly the Norwegian public had taken her to their hearts – the Princess had seemed slightly lacking in confidence and occasionally camera shy. This was compounded by a minor *faux pas* in protocol when, on departure, she forgot to turn and wave to her hosts on the steps of the Queen's Andover plane. However, all was forgiven two days later when, on 14 February, Buckingham Palace announced that the Prince and Princess of Wales were expecting their second child.

On arrival in Oslo, the Princess of Wales charmed the waiting crowds by chatting to children and receiving posies (above). At the ballet that evening the Princess was the focus of attention (far right); after the performance she met the principal ballerina with Crown Prince Harald and Princess Sonja (right). In the British Embassy gardens next morning Diana again showed her flair with children (next page)

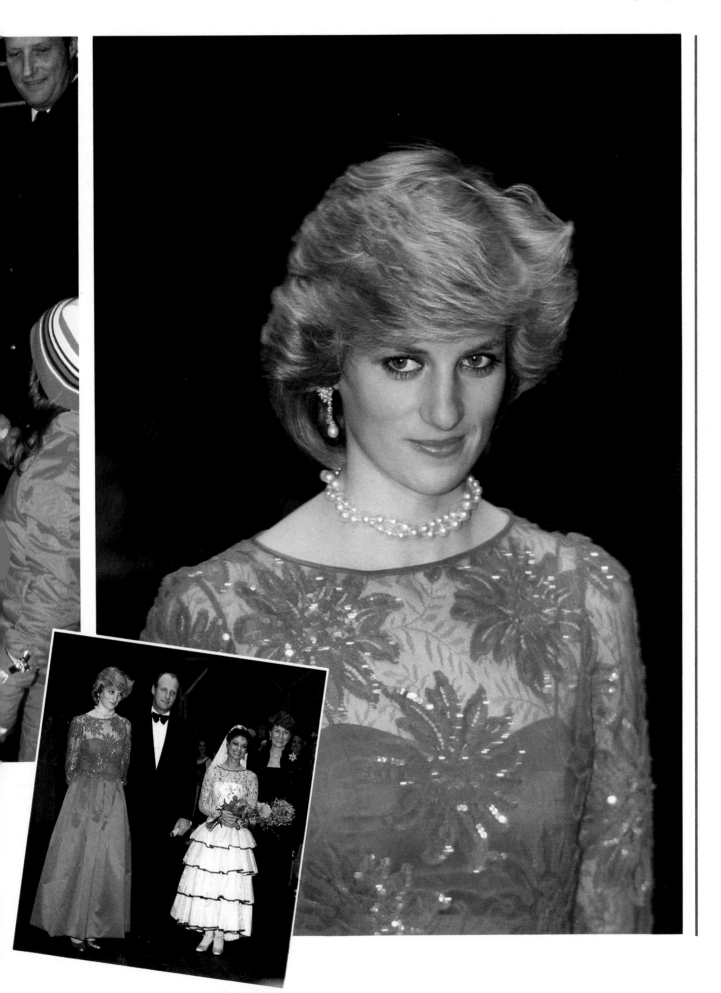

ANNE
IN AFRICA

Princess Anne's visit to Morocco, The Gambia and Upper Volta arose out of her strong personal commitment to deprived children everywhere. As president of the Save the Children Fund (SCF), she wanted to travel through some of the worst famine and drought-stricken areas in the world to promote the Fund's health and childcare programmes. The 10-day tour, in rigorous conditions of intense heat, rudimentary transport and primitive accommodation, was responsible for silencing many of Anne's harshest critics. She was at last given credit for being hard-working and concerned – with very much her own down-to-earth style.

She arrived in Africa to meet relief workers and inspect camps, villages and hospitals. As president of the Fund, she quickly showed that she was no mere figurehead. One SCF leader in Upper Volta reported: 'I couldn't believe it. I thought it would be just another public relations exercise. Instead, I was grilled in minute detail by someone who knew exactly what she was talking about.'

From the start, the Princess insisted on the minimum of fuss and ceremony. Despite the climate, she impressed everyone with her physical stamina as she pulled her weight in the desert, driving and hauling provisions. Her reaction to the plight of the children of Africa was practical and professional. Whether visiting a hospital deprived of penicillin for the previous four months, the Sahel region – where half the children under the age of five are expected to die – or areas where next year's crop was already in danger, she showed that her knowledge and involvement were genuine, and that she recognised that there were no easy, comfortable solutions. 'Money is not actually the answer,' she said. 'There is a limited amount we can do here. There is no point in swamping the area in manpower.' She further displayed her understanding of the Fund's awesome task by concluding: 'You can't do it all at once. You have to do it bit by bit.'

The tour had its lighter moments, however. In every community the Princess was fêted like an African Queen and showered with the gifts – grain, cooking pots and the traditional water carrier – that are usually presented by the village elders to a bride. But nothing could have been more gratifying than a huge chalked sign in one Gambian settlement: 'Welcome Princess Anne, we love our children.'

The tour of three African countries – from 15 to 25 February – was arduous and often uncomfortable for Princess Anne. Interspersed with ceremonial duties, such as (below) the Independence Day Parade at Banjul in The Gambia, were 10 days of visits to Save the Children Fund projects. The Princess rolled up her sleeves whenever possible (left, helping to pull the ferry across a Gambian river) and – with the temperature reaching 110° F (43° C) on occasions – showed her practical approach by wearing the right clothes for the job (far left, top and bottom, both in Upper Volta). For Princess Anne, who has always insisted that she is not 'a fairy Princess', the trip was a resounding success

CHARLES IN BRUNEI

For five days in February Prince Charles was present at the flamboyant festivities, held in the shadow of the gold-domed national mosque, with which the tiny sultanate of Brunei celebrated its independence from Britain. As the proceedings moved from the flag-waving and military marchpasts of the parade grounds to the Sultan's palace, Prince Charles was able to reflect on the fabulous wealth of one of the richest countries in the world. Although only 120 by 20 miles (193 by 32 kilometres) in area, Brunei virtually floats on a sea of oil and gas, a resource that yields £2500 million annually to the royal coffers. The recently completed New Istana palace, built at a cost of £300 million, is a breathtaking, Mogul-style construction of marble, mosaic and gold leaf. As well as being the most lavish – the domes at either end of the palace are solid gold – it is the largest royal residence in the world, with over 2000 rooms, including a throne room, mosque, sports complex, stables and heli-pad.

The banquet room, where Prince Charles sat down with 20 foreign Heads of State and 3000 other dignitaries, is just as monumental: high, gold-leafed walls, vaulted, inlaid ceilings and the largest chandeliers in the world. As Sultan Sir Hassanal Bolkiah presided over his country's most important ever State occasion, his assembled guests were served Malaysian delicacies from silver tureens so large that each needed two men to lift the lid.

Brunei's five-day independence extravaganza, with its succession of parades, ceremonies, firework displays and vast banquets, posed the country considerable problems of security and accommodation for its illustrious guests. The Sultan's solution was to pack the normally tranquil capital of Bandar Seri Begawan with bodyguards and to build special apartments for his visitors. Prince Charles – as representative of the Queen – was particularly well looked after, being housed in an elegant lodge, complete with swimming pool. During the opening celebrations, Charles sat on the royal dais in the position of honour next to the Sultan, where, dressed in open-necked naval whites, he chatted to Bolkiah's two Muslim wives. The Prince also visited Brunei's Gurkha regiment as its commander-in-chief, and enjoyed a tour of the capital's Churchill Museum. Finally, just hours before Prince Charles's scheduled departure, he and the Sultan joined forces to play on the same side in a game of polo – it seemed the perfect parting of the ways for an old empire and a new nation.

The links between Britain and Brunei, which ended officially on 1 January 1984, go back to a 19th-century agreement in which the UK undertook to control the South East Asian country's defence and foreign affairs. In recognition of this, the present Sultan laid on a lavish display of royal pageantry for Prince Charles's arrival. The Prince then chatted to school children (left and far left) who presented him with their pictures of the royal family. Also a fervent anglophile is the Sultan's father, Sir Muda Omar Ali Saifuddin (above, with Prince Charles), who founded the capital's Churchill Museum. Many of the Independence – or 'Merdeka' – celebrations were held in the new palace, which contains a magnificent throne room (inset top). It has four carved thrones and 12 two-tonne chandeliers, and can accommodate 2000 people. In total, the five days of festivities cost the Sultan of Brunei nearly £13 million

THE QUEEN MOTHER IN WEST GERMANY

At the British Military Hospital in Münster the Queen Mother, looking especially pretty in shades of pink and lilac (centre left), received a bouquet from five-year-old Louise Tennuci and her sister Amanda (left). The following day, St Patrick's Day, the royal visitor distributed shamrock and then presented medals for long service and good conduct to men of the 1st Battalion Irish Guards, suitably adorned (far left). Later in the day the Queen Mother spent some time with members of the warrant officers' and sergeants' mess and posed for a formal photograph (below)

Many of the royal family's engagements are connected with their involvement with the armed forces, and the Queen Mother's brief visit to Münster, West Germany, in mid-March was one of these. In her capacity as colonel-in-chief of the Royal Army Medical Corps she visited the British Military Hospital on the afternoon of Friday, 16 March, and on the following morning attended the Irish Guards' St Patrick's Day parade and presented shamrock to the regiment.

On her arrival at the hospital the Queen Mother, wearing a dusky pink coat and toning lilac hat with a veil, was presented with a bouquet by the two young daughters of the Irish Guards' regimental sergeant major. Accompanied by the commanding officer of the regiment she then toured the hospital wards and watched preparations for an exercise to test the hospital's role in wartime. Before leaving, the Queen Mother presented the hospital with a memento of her visit – a photograph of herself, personally signed.

Saturday dawned bright but cold for the St Patrick's Day parade by the Irish Guards, one of the seven regiments of the Household Division; appropriately, it was formed in 1900, the year the Queen Mother was born. The parade dates from 1902 and has been held annually since then. Even in wartime the Irish Guards have maintained the tradition. In 1944, shortly after the Allied landings at Anzio in Italy, they held the parade near Sorrento and a year later, a week before crossing the Rhine, they paraded at Nijmegen in Holland. In 1967 Field Marshal Earl Alexander flew out specially to distribute the shamrock at the St Patrick's Day parade of the 1st Battalion, then serving in Aden.

On this most recent occasion the Queen Mother, who first attended the ceremony in 1928, was greeted by a royal salute on her arrival and presented with a spray of shamrock. She then handed baskets of the Irish national emblem to five company commanders for distribution among the men, and personally presented shamrock to the officers. After three cheers were given for the royal visitor the commanding officer, Lieutenant Colonel Sean O'Dwyer, led the regimental marchpast. At the conclusion of the parade the Queen Mother presented medals and visited the warrant officers' and sergeants' mess where she watched a display of Irish dancing by the regiment's junior dance team, and posed for a formal photograph. Her final engagement consisted of a visit to the junior ranks' dining room where she was 'toasted' by one of the longest serving soldiers of the regiment.

THE QUEEN IN JORDAN

The State visit to Jordan by the Queen in the last week of March was described by *The Times* as 'the most dangerous and diplomatically sensitive tour of her reign'. Jordan, a pro-Western moderate Arab nation, is involved in the turbulence of Middle East politics and the long-standing struggle between Arab and Jew. It has strong and historic links with Britain, which supports King Hussein's efforts to reach agreement with Israel over the establishment of a separate homeland for Palestinian refugees.

The visit nearly did not go ahead. Just two days before the Queen and Prince Philip were due to arrive a bomb exploded outside the Inter-Continental Hotel in Amman, the capital – the work of guerrillas opposed to Hussein's policies. Later the same day another explosive device was defused nearby. Officials in London met hurriedly to assess the situation but decided the visit should proceed – which it did, albeit under the tightest security of any British royal tour.

On their arrival in Jordan on Monday 26 March the Queen and Prince Philip were met by the 48-year-old King, a direct descendant of the Prophet Muhammad, and his 32-year-old American-born wife, Queen Noor. The official party then drove at speed to the Basman Palace via a route devoid of crowds and patrolled by police, troops and security personnel. They were closely escorted by Bedouin guards in a convoy of Land-Rovers fitted front and rear with 50mm Browning machine-guns. In a speech that night during a glittering banquet the Queen referred to 'the tragedy that has befallen the Palestinian people' and told Hussein that 'the world has been deeply impressed by your efforts in the face of many discouragements and setbacks to achieve a negotiated settlement of the problems of the Middle East.'

The main event the next day was a visit to the royal stud farm at Hunnar where some of the royal stables' 80 Arab mares and stallions were paraded in front of the visitors. Before she left, the Queen was presented with a magnificently embroidered Bedouin saddle fringed with tassels.

On Wednesday the Queen and Prince Philip were driven by King Hussein to a farm in the Jordan Valley within sight of the Israeli-occupied town of Jericho on the West Bank. There followed a picnic on the shores of the Dead Sea where refreshments were taken in a specially erected tent.

The schedule for Thursday included a roam around the ruins of the ancient city of Petra, followed in the afternoon by a few hours' sailing in the Red Sea off Aqaba in the King's yacht.

On Friday the Queen and Prince Philip boarded their Tri-Star jet (which was equipped with anti-missile devices) for the flight home. For some in the official party it had been a tense and worrying five days, yet throughout it all the Queen and Prince Philip had appeared to be their usual relaxed selves, as if there was nothing at all to worry about.

On her first evening the Queen was guest of honour at a banquet hosted by King Hussein at the Basman Palace (left). The two monarchs are old friends; they were both crowned in 1953. An undoubted highlight of the visit was the trip to the 2000-year-old city of Petra, once the capital of the Nabataean people and a flourishing trading centre, the ruins of which were discovered in 1812. The Queen was taken to see the tombs, cut out of rock, which are now used as dwellings (top). During the tour Prince Philip was often escorted by Queen Noor (above), who married King Hussein in 1978

One of the most highly charged events of this politically sensitive visit was the occasion when the Queen laid a wreath to Arab soldiers killed fighting against Israel. On her arrival at the memorial she was accompanied by a military guard (right). Throughout the five-day tour security was extremely tight; the routes travelled by official cars were empty save for soldiers patrolling with submachine-guns (below). On the third day the royal visitors were taken by King Hussein for a picnic on the shores of the Dead Sea, where they were able to look across to the Israeli-occupied West Bank (bottom right), captured from Jordan in the Six Day War of June 1967. As Jordanian military helicopters droned overhead, Israeli jets could be heard on patrol not far away

At the royal stud at Hunnar, on the outskirts of Amman, the Queen and Prince Philip were shown around by Princess Aliya, who runs the stables (top). Another engagement that clearly delighted the Queen was a meeting, at her request, with members of the British community in Amman (above). The occasion was notable for the friendly, relaxed atmosphere – and the beaming faces of children keen to get as near as possible to their Queen

STATE VISIT OF THE EMIR OF BAHRAIN

The fact that the Emir of Bahrain paid a State visit to Windsor Castle rather than Buckingham Palace emphasised the strongly personal nature of the event. On his arrival at Home Park, Windsor, the Emir took the salute during a marchpast by royal Guardsmen (top left). The Queen and her guest then drove to Windsor Castle in the State Landau built for King Edward VII in 1902 (left). This splendid carriage, decorated in gold leaf and with crimson satin upholstery, is used by the Queen to meet foreign Heads of State; it also conveyed Prince Charles and his bride to Buckingham Palace after their marriage at St Paul's in 1981. During his stay at the castle the Emir, himself a noted horse-breeder, was shown round the royal mews by Prince Philip (top centre). Towards the end of his four-day visit the Emir invited members of the royal family, peers, politicians, diplomats and businessmen to a sumptuous banquet at a top hotel in Mayfair. Two of the guests were Princess Alexandra and Lord Whitelaw (top right)

Today many royal Heads of State are primarily figureheads, but there still exist royal rulers who wield extensive personal powers. One of these is the Emir of Bahrain, who paid a State visit to Windsor Castle from 10 to 13 April. The Emir, Sheikh Isa Bin-Sulman al-Khalifah, is Head of State in a nation of 350,000 people, a former British protectorate located between Qatar and Saudi Arabia that achieved full independence from Britain in 1971. The visit was not just an official occasion – it also provided an opportunity for the Emir to renew his acquaintance with the Queen, a long-time friend.

The personal significance of the visit was demonstrated when the 51-year-old Emir arrived from Heathrow airport at the Royal Pavilion in Home Park, Windsor, for a fully ceremonial State welcome – the first given by the Queen at Windsor for 10 years. There to greet him were also Prince Philip and Prime Minister Margaret Thatcher. After inspecting a guard of honour formed by men from the Coldstream Guards, the Emir drove the short distance to the castle in the 1902 State Landau, the richly decorated carriage used for visits by foreign rulers. Waiting to greet him were the Prince and Princess of Wales, Princess Margaret and other members of the royal family. That evening the prime minister and the Archbishop of Canterbury were among many distinguished guests who attended a sparkling State banquet at the castle.

Next day the Queen and Prince Philip escorted the Emir to an exhibition on royalty and railways organised by Madame Tussaud's museum at Windsor station, opposite the castle. From there the Emir was whisked to London for talks with Mrs Thatcher and lunch at Number 10 Downing Street.

A banquet at the Guildhall in the City of London emphasised the strong commercial links between the two countries. Oil, which provides about 75 per cent of Bahrain's revenue, figured prominently in official discussions as did security in the Middle East, particularly in view of the Gulf War between Iran and Iraq. Anxiety on this last matter was raised in talks held on the Friday between Sheikh Muhammad Bin-Mubarak al-Khalifah, Bahrain's minister of foreign affairs, and Sir Geoffrey Howe. Later that day the Emir and his advisors said their goodbyes to their royal hosts and departed, having reinforced personal friendships and strengthened the bonds of amity between two nations with historic links.

ANDREW
IN LOS ANGELES

When Prince Andrew donned a red baseball cap at a reception party – to the laughter of onlookers – his visit to Los Angeles (from 15 to 19 April) looked set fair to rival the success of the Queen's Californian tour the year before. Esconced in the plushest suite of the renowned Beverly Wilshire hotel the Prince enjoyed the finest of American hospitality. A colourful Mexican band greeted his arrival and the hotel management had even flown in crates of Guinness and pale ale for royal consumption. However, all else that followed was overshadowed by a controversy that undoubtedly soured the trip and gave the Press ample ammunition to dent the reputation of the Prince. The paint-spraying incident at a housing project in the Los Angeles black ghetto of Watts, where attendant photographers claimed Andrew deliberately aimed a spray gun and showered them with white emulsion paint, was certainly unfortunate if not irresponsible. The ensuing storm of outraged headlines and recriminations over damaged equipment did its best to stigmatise the whole tour as a national disgrace. The near-hysteria can be largely explained by the fact that the young, charismatic Prince is particularly newsworthy; his relationship with the Press has always been volatile, so when a practical joke backfired they were ready to pounce. But the incident was hardly unprecedented – in 1959 Prince Philip soaked photographers at the Chelsea Flower Show with a garden hose.

Although some took the opportunity to carp at every turn, the rest of Andrew's five-day stay passed off smoothly, with many engagements tailored to suit his interests. As a pilot himself, he clearly enjoyed a visit to a San Diego helicopter base, and on his inspections of a space laboratory and a photographic museum the Prince won over the crowds with his usual open charm and broad smile. It was on a tour of the MGM studios where the sequel to 2001 – A Space Odyssey was being shot that Prince Andrew, aware of the pressure on him, replied to a question with an ironic grin that he would not like to be a film star.

Apart from attending functions on behalf of the British Olympic Association, Prince Andrew helped to boost home exports by meeting tradesmen and shop-owners taking part in the Britain Salutes Beverly Hills celebrations. He also found time for more informal pleasures, sampling a downtown show and providing a glamorous dance partner for the young ladies of a Gordonstoun School benefit evening.

Early in the tour Prince Andrew told an audience that part of the aim of the visit was to show Americans that the British people were not just 'cute-accented traditionalists'. Whatever else he did, he certainly did that.

What was originally planned as a private visit for Prince Andrew turned into a very public and hectic round of engagements. At a fund-raising banquet for the British Olympic Association, guests paid $1000 a head to dine with the Prince. Afterwards, British expatriates presented Andrew with a caricature of himself (above, with Dudley Moore – supporting the picture – and a tie-less Tom Jones). At a San Diego airbase he enjoyed the chance to pilot a helicopter (right). During his more formal duties Andrew collected a number of hats, including a red baseball cap and (left) an outsize sombrero

THE QUEEN IN WEST GERMANY

While being a stickler for discipline, the Queen always takes a keen personal interest in the welfare of her servicemen and their families and loves to be shown their latest equipment and manoeuvres (left, below and below left). The impressive triumphal arch (above) mounted to mark the Queen's visit to the Royal Regiment of Artillery at Dortmund is made up entirely of M109 self-propelled guns – triumphal arches of weapons (usually swords) are very popular with the armed forces

Reviews and inspections of the armed forces account for a large part of the royal family's duties. The Queen is colonel-in-chief (or captain-general) of 22 British regiments and corps and her tours of inspection take her as far afield as Germany – where she went on 22 May for a private visit to regiments of the British Army of the Rhine. Because this was a private visit the Queen had no official reception from the German authorities other than a formal welcome from German dignitaries when she landed at Essen-Mülheim in the industrial Ruhr region. (The last time she had paid a private visit to British troops in Germany was in 1977, the year of her Silver Jubilee.) During her visit, she met servicemen and their families from the Royal Artillery Regiment of which she is captain-general and the Royal Greenjackets of which she is colonel-in-chief.

The Queen was driven to Dortmund, headquarters of the Army's Artillery Division, and during a reception held in her honour there, attended by the mayor, she signed the city's Golden Book. At Centaur House, Napier Barracks, where she was to stay during her visit, Lieutenant-General Sir Martin Farndale, the corps commander, and Lady Farndale gave a banquet for the Queen. The next day she inspected the imposing array of guns and equipment drawn up on the parade ground. Fourteen regiments each paraded 18 guns, howitzers or missile systems, plus a composite unit of blowpipe batteries and a saluting battery from 3rd Regiment Royal Horse Artillery. In her address, the Queen expressed her pleasure to be with her regiment in Dortmund, the largest gunner garrison in the world, and to see, on display for the first time, all the royal artillery weapons based in Germany. The Queen then officially opened the Anglo-German riding school at Napier Barracks and watched six disabled German children take part in an indoor riding display. This was followed by an inspection of equipment. The Queen then moved on to a regimental activities exhibition in which each gunner regiment had a stand demonstrating some aspect of its life in Germany. That evening, after attending a military concert, the Queen had dinner in the officers' mess of 22nd Air Defence Regiment and, on her departure, the route back to Centaur House was lined by gunners holding burning torches.

The next day, the Queen flew to Celle near Hanover to visit the Royal Greenjackets. On her arrival she was greeted by the commander of the West German 16th Air Regiment (*Luftwaffe*) as well as senior British officers. At Celle she watched military manoeuvres and a display of the duties of a rifleman in the 1980s. This was followed by a meeting with the local dignitaries in the Rathaus (town hall) where the Queen signed another Golden Book.

THE QUEEN MOTHER IN THE CHANNEL ISLANDS

The three-day visit to the Channel Islands at the end of May by the Queen Mother was delightfully different from the usual royal round, not only because of the imaginative itinerary but also because of the picturesque setting. Located between 50 and 100 miles (80 and 160 kilometres) off Weymouth, between the coasts of England and France, the Channel Islands have had close associations with both England and Normandy since the Norman Conquest, and were keenly contested between the two countries for centuries. Annexed to the Crown of England in the 13th century, the islands today are self-governing British Crown dependencies; they do not form part of the United Kingdom. The main islands are Jersey, Guernsey, Sark and Alderney; the total area of 75 square miles (195 square kilometres) sustains a population of 133,000 – most of Norman stock.

For the Queen Mother the occasion evoked nostalgic memories of the visit she made with King George VI in 1945, shortly after the islands' liberation from five years of Nazi occupation. On Alderney she signed a visitors' book on the same table on which the Germans had signed their formal surrender 39 years before.

Everywhere the Queen Mother was welcomed with warmth and affection. The arrival of the royal yacht *Britannia* at St Peter Port, Guernsey, was marked by the thunder of cannon from the medieval Castle Cornet that overlooks the harbour. During a two-hour drive along cobblestone streets the Queen Mother's progress was eagerly followed by wellwishers along the route. On Sark, however, where motor cars are forbidden, she travelled down dirt roads by horse-drawn carriage, accompanied by the Seigneur, the island's governor. It is a place far removed from the modern world; on her arrival the welcoming parade included a fire engine hauled by tractor and firefighters sporting Edwardian-style helmets.

In the course of her visit the Queen Mother called at an old people's home, showed children at a youth centre how to play pool, dropped into a school, planted a tree at a newly-opened community centre, watched a fireworks display and, on her final evening, hosted a banquet aboard *Britannia*. Throughout the tour the Channel Islanders' affection had been expressed by gift upon gift of freshly-cut flowers. And at St Saviours on Guernsey the royal visitor drove beneath an overhead banner that succinctly proclaimed the feelings of the population: 'Queen Mother, We All Love You.'

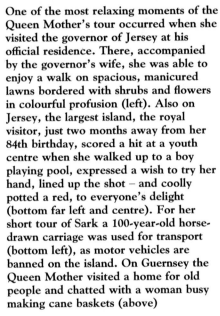

One of the most relaxing moments of the Queen Mother's tour occurred when she visited the governor of Jersey at his official residence. There, accompanied by the governor's wife, she was able to enjoy a walk on spacious, manicured lawns bordered with shrubs and flowers in colourful profusion (left). Also on Jersey, the largest island, the royal visitor, just two months away from her 84th birthday, scored a hit at a youth centre when she walked up to a boy playing pool, expressed a wish to try her hand, lined up the shot – and coolly potted a red, to everyone's delight (bottom far left and centre). For her short tour of Sark a 100-year-old horse-drawn carriage was used for transport (bottom left), as motor vehicles are banned on the island. On Guernsey the Queen Mother visited a home for old people and chatted with a woman busy making cane baskets (above)

ANNE AT THE OLYMPIC GAMES

Princess Anne's lengthy visit to the 23rd Olympiad in Los Angeles, from 27 July to 12 August, was the culmination of eight months' hard work in her capacity as president of the British Olympic Association. Throughout the year she attended dozens of receptions, concerts, banquets and gala events – including the Sports Ball at the Grosvenor House Hotel and an evening at Number 10 Downing Street – in active support of the money-raising activities of the British Olympic Appeal Fund. In January, Anne had spent five days in the USA, first in New Orleans, Louisiana, and then in Houston, Texas, linking up with the chairman of the British Olympic Association USA, Tony Thompson, to boost the appeal and meet oilmen and ranchers. Her next trip abroad was a little less formal, travelling as a spectator to the 14th Winter Olympic Games in Sarajevo, Yugoslavia. There, as well as enjoying an exhilarating bobsleigh ride, she witnessed the record-breaking, gold-medal performances of Britain's ice dancers, Jane Torvill and Christopher Dean.

As a former competitor and veteran participant of the 1976 Montreal Games, Princess Anne was able to watch the British team's Los Angeles effort with an experienced eye. Although Anne took in a wide spectrum of events, as a horsewoman she particularly appreciated the successes of the British equestrian team, who picked up three medals: a silver and a bronze for Three-Day Eventing and an individual bronze for Virginia Holgate. While at the Games, Anne was involved in two mild controversies – one irritating to the Princess and the other amusing. The first surrounded Press reports that she and her husband, Mark Phillips – present at the Olympics as a commentator for Australian television's Channel 10 – would be staying in separate hotels, so supposedly adding fuel to the stories of a rift in their marriage. 'Oh no, not again,' was Mark's reaction. The simple fact of the matter was that Captain Phillips was contractually bound to reside in the same $65-a-night Holiday Inn as the rest of his broadcasting team. Anne, meanwhile, occupied the whole of the fourth floor of the palatial Huntington Sheraton in Pasadena, sharing a three-bedroomed, three-bathroomed suite with Prince Philip and a lady-in-waiting. The second incident centred on some joking comments made by Britain's Decathlon gold medallist, Daley Thompson. After being asked at a Press conference whether he would like to have children, he had cheekily intimated that he would – and that their mother might be the Princess. In the furore that followed Anne defended the joke by saying she had not been offended in the slightest and that the criticism of Thompson was 'absurd'. Nothing, she added, should be allowed to detract from his 'brilliant achievement'.

As president of the British Olympic Association, Princess Anne's first appearance as a spectator was at the Winter Games in Sarajevo, Yugoslavia. There she met Britain's ice-skating heroes, Torvill and Dean, after their gold medal dance performance (right). At the Summer Games in Los Angeles Anne was eager to watch as many British athletes in action as possible. She was particularly pleased to witness the rare success of Britain's hockey team, who brought back a bronze medal (far right, during the vital game for third place). After Daley Thompson had carried off the Decathlon gold medal for the second Olympics in succession, Anne was among the first on the track to congratulate him (above)

CHARLES IN PAPUA NEW GUINEA

'Wuroh, wuroh, wuroh, all man meri bilong Manus. Mi hammamas tru.' ('Thank you all men and women of Manus. I am truly filled with happiness.') With these carefully spoken words of Pidjin, Prince Charles brandished a spear and accepted his new position as leader of the people of Manus Island.

It was almost the end of the Prince's five-day visit to Papua New Guinea in August. The main reason for the visit had been to open the new Parliament building in the capital, Port Moresby, on the 7th, the day after his arrival. The next day, at Popondetta, the Prince was formally appointed colonel-in-chief of the Royal Pacific Islands Regiment and, in turn, presented new colours to the regiment's 2nd Battalion. But it was the day spent on Manus Island that provided the most colourful events of the tour.

The Prince had arrived on the island – some 220 miles (354 kilometres) across the South Pacific from Papua New Guinea – on a ceremonial outrigger canoe, flanked by warriors in dugouts. Carried ashore on a carved wooden bed – a *keyau* – he was greeted by island MP Mrs Nahau Rooney who, dressed in grass skirt, beads and a rooster-feather head-dress, placed a welcoming garland around his neck. He was then escorted by chanting local girls up the gleaming beach, along a carpet of dried palm leaves, to the initiation hut. This hut was traditionally used by island elders to teach young men the facts of life and their martial duties as warriors, but in this instance the Prince of Wales was allowed to sit outside and await the next move.

Against a backdrop of mangroves and lagoons, the ceremony began. Seated still on his *keyau*, and surrounded by singing, painted warriors, clicking shells and beating their shields, Prince Charles was adorned with dogs' teeth necklaces, a headband and a basket containing a lime pot – all symbols of his new status. A lower chief then danced forward wielding a spear and tomahawk and boomed: 'We call on you to take this spear, so that we can be protected in time of war.' In accepting the spear, to the roars of 'Wuroh!' from the thousands of islanders lining Lorengau beach and wedged in the branches of the banyan trees, Prince Charles duly became the Lapan of Manus, or High Chief.

Under the cloudless tropical sky, the day's ceremonies reached a climax in a wild, gyrating dance to rhythmic drumbeats – putting the seal on one of the most vibrant and exotic engagements the Prince of Wales is ever likely to experience.

In a ceremony at Popondetta on the mainland of Papua New Guinea, Prince Charles was made the first colonel-in-chief of the Royal Pacific Regiment (opposite page). He apologised for not wearing the correct uniform, explaining that he had not had time to procure the right one – instead he wore the uniform of the 2nd Gurkhas. Afterwards, Charles was presented with a spear, which he used to hack down a 90-lb (41-kilogram) palm-oil nut from a tree (left, bottom). Charles's arrival on Lorengau beach, Manus Island, mirrored that of Captain Philip Carteret of the Royal Navy, who, in 1776, landed and named the islet 'Admiralty Island'. On Manus, Charles received the title of High Chief of Manus or 'Lapan'. After being draped with dogs' teeth necklaces – the teeth were once currency on the island – he was fitted with a woven headband, complete with Union Jack and local flag designs (centre left). The next stage for the Prince – or 'Nambawan pikinini bilong Missis Kwin', as he is known in Pidjin – was the presentation of a Manus basket made from stripped tree-bark, which he wore over his left shoulder (left). Finally, as a symbol of his obligation to maintain peace and order, he took possession of an ornately carved spear, tipped with obsidian. As well as defending his new people, Charles's responsibilities as Lapan are to distribute wealth and give occasional feasts. His privileges include being able to wear the dogs' teeth at official functions (and even trade some of the teeth for sacks of sago should he fall on hard times) and hang shells on his house and canoe – and the right to insult any of his subjects should he disagree with them. The new Lapan of Manus (previous page) was also presented with the recognised sign of welcome, a bunch of betel nuts – a mild stimulant with the unfortunate side-effect of staining the mouth red. Prince Charles brought back a model canoe for William, which he told the islanders the young Prince 'will no doubt break immediately; he's at a very dangerous age.' And for the royal household there were string bags, a carved coffee table and a wooden crocodile

CHARLES IN THE NETHERLANDS

To the 2000 grey-haired veterans, dressed in red berets, with their medals glinting on their chests, it was a poignant moment. As the Prince of Wales, commander-in-chief of the Parachute Regiment, laid a wreath of poppies in the Oosterbeek military cemetery, their minds were cast back 40 years to the bloody and ultimately disastrous Battle of Arnhem. Against huge odds they and their compatriots had been dropped behind enemy lines to take the Rhine bridges; eight days of ferocious fighting narrowly failed to achieve the objective and, having sustained heavy losses, the Allied forces withdrew. After Prince Charles had laid his wreath, others laid theirs: Queen Beatrix and Prince Klaus of the Netherlands, the ambassadors of the wartime Allies, and many of the veterans and their commanders. Finally, in a tribute to the 1747 Allied British and Polish troops buried in the cemetery, local children laid a wreath on each grave.

The ceremony, held on Sunday 23 September 1984, was an emotional climax to a week of remembrance and reunion. A few days before, 60 paratroopers had dropped from Hercules planes to make a landing on the same patch of scrubland that had marked the start of Operation Market Garden on 17 September 1944; and the now 82-year-old Major-General Urquhart, commander of the 1st British Airborne Division at Arnhem, had presented a sword representing the 'spirit of resistance' to the southern Dutch people of Gelderland, who had suffered savage reprisals for the failure of the attack. Despite the presence of royalty the week belonged to the veterans, some now infirm or confined to wheelchairs, who had travelled from as far afield as North America and Australia to be there.

The Prince of Wales, as commander-in-chief of the Parachute Regiment (above), attended a day of remembrance for the 40th anniversary of the Battle of Arnhem. At the ceremony in the Oosterbeek military cemetery (left), he was joined by Queen Beatrix of the Netherlands (far left). Afterwards, he talked to veterans of the battle (below)

THE QUEEN IN CANADA

The 21-gun salute accorded to the Queen and Prince Philip on their arrival in Moncton, New Brunswick, on 21 September proclaimed the beginning of the 15-day royal tour of Canada, whose countryside was already bursting with the first reds and yellows of a characteristically spectacular autumn. The predominantly French province of New Brunswick was celebrating its bicentenary, and the festivities there – which included French-Arcadian folk songs from schoolchildren and a visit to Shediac, a town famous for its lobsters – were the first taste of a hectic two weeks of ceremonies, gala performances, dinners, presentations, openings, walkabouts and military pageantry.

After three days in New Brunswick, culminating in a glittering banquet given by the provincial premier, Mr Richard Hatfield, the royal couple flew to Ottawa, the country's capital, to a welcome from the honour guard of the 22nd Royal Regiment. After a trip in an open landau to Government house – where two years previously she had proclaimed Canada's new Constitution – the Queen made a speech on the virtues of Parliamentary democracy.

Travelling (and staying overnight on board) whenever possible on the royal yacht *Britannia*, the Queen and Prince Philip then moved to Toronto for four days where, along with a crowd of 50,000 enthusiastic spectators, they enjoyed one of the largest military pageants in Canadian history – nine marching bands and 1300 soldiers. There was a brief scare during the procession that preceded the show, when the horses drawing the royal landau reared up, frightened by the 21-gun salute. The Queen, however, calmly transferred to a jeep and carried on without turning a hair. The programme for the Queen's last day in Toronto was packed: it included opening a new convention centre, a hospital tour, unveiling plaques and wreaths and, finally, a lunch to celebrate the 150th anniversary of the province of Ontario. Prince Philip returned to Britain on 4 October and the Queen completed the last leg of the tour on her own. In Winnipeg in the province of Manitoba she attended, among many other engagements, a dedication ceremony at the Tri-Service monument, and the Royal Manitoba Festival, which featured the Winnipeg Symphony Orchestra and the Royal Ballet.

Opening an Aviation Museum on 7 October was the last of some 70 engagements. In 15 exhausting days the Queen had criss-crossed the country – often flying four times a day to take in some of the smaller towns – to be greeted everywhere she went by the vociferously patriotic Canadian public, to whom the royal visit represented a chance to celebrate their own traditional links with the Crown.

On her departure, the Queen flew to Kentucky, USA, for a private visit to the world's most famous horse-breeding centre.

In the Canadians' response to the Queen's tour royal pomp and splendour were combined with ceremonies recalling the country's past. In Toronto the Queen visited Parliament House (left), where she spoke on the virtues of democracy. At Fort Wellington, Ontario, a loyalist battle was re-enacted in period costume (below). At Brantford, Ontario, the Queen visited the Six Nations Reserve, meeting Mohawk Chief Wellington Stass (above). When she left Winnipeg local dignitaries escorted the Queen to her plane (below left)

On 3 July 1984 the Queen attended a Service of Installation of the Knights of the Thistle in St Giles's Cathedral, Edinburgh (left). It was one of the highlights of a week of royal engagements carried out in the Scottish capital and its environs

Part III
THE ROYAL CALENDAR

Many of the functions undertaken by the royal family are dictated by tradition and affairs of State. The pageantry and ritual of royal ceremonies provide a colourful link with the past, and underline the continuity of government and national pride. The regular round of royal duties also enables the modern monarchy to be seen at work, travelling the country, meeting the people and promoting public support for the institution itself.

The royal year begins and ends in Norfolk at the Queen's private estate, Sandringham, just down the road from Diana's birthplace. There, in this favoured retreat of broad lawns, ornamental lakes and beautifully landscaped gardens, the Queen and her family are able to relax, delighting in the pleasure of the unhurried pace of rural life, and enjoying plenty of riding.

In February, the Queen returns to London. There are engagements and invitations to be discussed and slotted into the diary; there are also investitures to be conducted and a stream of meetings with personal and government advisors.

For the Queen one of the most enjoyable regular engagements comes in early April when she and the rest of the family attend the three-day Badminton horse trials in the beautiful Cotswold countryside. In 1984 this occasion was overshadowed by the death earlier in the year of the Duke of Beaufort, founder of the trials. The duke had been the Queen's Master of the Horse and a great personal friend – almost a father figure – and his loss was deeply mourned.

The day before Good Friday the Queen distributes the Royal Maundy. This ancient tradition, dating from the 12th century, was performed in 1984 in Southwell Minster, Nottinghamshire. After the service the Queen travelled to Windsor Castle for Easter.

Over the past few years the Queen Mother has begun her own tradition about this time by making an annual visit to France to stay with close friends such as the Rothschilds. She usually makes a point, however, of returning to Britain in time for the Queen's birthday on 21 April, a very private affair spent, whenever possible, at Windsor.

Windsor Castle is also, of course, the preferred destination for the Queen and Prince Philip on their 'free' weekends, while down the road in Windsor Great Park stands Royal Lodge, the Queen Mother's weekend retreat where Princess Margaret and Lady Sarah Armstrong-Jones are regular guests.

In May the Chelsea Flower Show in London attracts many thousands of visitors – including royalty. For the Queen, the Queen Mother and Princess Margaret the great exhibition of flowers and shrubs in the massive marquee, and the ingenuity of the model gardens, make this a fascinating occasion, when they can examine at leisure the new varieties on display and admire many flowers named after them.

By mid-summer, sporting and social engagements dot the royal diary. Prince Charles's polo season is under way (he often plays several times a week), and the Royal Windsor Horse Show allows Prince Philip the chance to demonstrate his skill at carriage-driving, the younger royals, from little Zara Phillips to Lady Helen Windsor, cheering from the sidelines.

Resplendent in their tall black bearskins and scarlet jackets, Prince Charles and Prince Philip (above) took part in the 1984 Trooping the Colour, when the Grenadier Guards were the featured regiment. The ceremony takes place on Horse Guards Parade

The Chelsea Flower Show and Royal Ascot are two of the regular annual events that the royal family attend with obvious enjoyment. At Chelsea in 1984 the Prince and Princess of Wales paused to admire a display of pansies (top), while at Royal Ascot, the Queen Mother looked appealing in a flower-trimmed hat and toning coat (above)

For Royal Ascot the family arrive at the course in horse-drawn carriages and watch the races from the comfort of the royal box. At this time the Queen usually invites a few old friends to Windsor for the week.

In 1984 the Queen's official birthday was celebrated on Saturday 16 June, when, riding side-saddle, the Queen took the salute at her birthday parade. Trooping the Colour in 1984 was also the last working royal duty of Sefton, one of the horses seriously injured by an IRA bomb in 1982. When the Queen and her family appeared on the balcony of Buckingham Palace after Trooping the Colour to watch the flypast of jets, Prince William made his first appearance there. Much to the delight of the crowds below, Prince Charles lifted him up for a better view.

On 4 August members of the immediate royal family do their best to be in London for the Queen Mother's birthday, which she celebrates at a Clarence House lunch with close friends and relations.

As soon as possible after her birthday the Queen Mother flies up to her favourite refuge, the Castle of Mey on the northernmost tip of Scotland, where she spends three weeks. Meanwhile, the Queen, Peter and Zara Phillips and a few other close members of the family will have boarded *Britannia* for the cruise to Balmoral via the Western Isles and Aberdeen. By mid-August the Queen is installed in Balmoral for her summer holiday.

After this Highland interlude, it is back to Buckingham Palace and the normal round of investitures, meetings, dinners and other engagements. On 6 November, glittering with diamonds, the Queen drove to Westminster by horse-drawn coach in the traditional grand procession of liveried footmen and postilions to open the new session of Parliament. Five days later the Queen and Prince Philip turned out for a more sombre annual event, the laying of wreaths at the Cenotaph on Remembrance Sunday. The Annual Royal Variety Performance, also in November, was a sparkling occasion much enjoyed by the royal visitors.

Just before Christmas Day, the royal family assemble at Windsor Castle. On Christmas Eve, after a service held in St George's Chapel, the family open their Christmas presents. Christmas day itself is devoted to another service, followed by a Christmas lunch and then plenty of fireside games. Two or three days later, as the extended family leave Windsor to go their separate ways, the Queen and some of her close family depart for Sandringham and the New Year.

MAUNDY THURSDAY

Based on the ritual of the Last Supper, the Royal Maundy ceremony used to involve washing the feet of the poor and distributing food and clothing. Now the Queen donates alms, in the form of specially minted coins, to men and women over the age of 65 chosen for their worthiness rather than their poverty. The amount given equals in pence the age of the sovereign, and the number of recipients also corresponds to the sovereign's age.

Four orphans, as usual, also received the Maundy money at the ceremony held at Southwell Minster, Nottinghamshire in 1984 (far left); nosegays were once thought to protect against disease. Yeomen of the Guard carry the gold dishes bearing the Maundy money (left); the Maundy recipients receive a red purse containing £5.50 (in place of food and clothing) and a white one containing the Maundy money (above)

THE CHELSEA FLOWER SHOW

Held by the Royal Horticultural Society in the grounds of the Royal Hospital (home of the Chelsea Pensioners), the Chelsea Flower Show in May is the highlight of the gardener's calendar. The Queen and other members of the royal family usually pay a private visit on the Monday afternoon (which in 1984 fell on 21 May) before the show opens. Outstanding exhibits in this show included *Amateur Gardening*'s Victorian villa garden (to mark the magazine's centenary); a series of terrace house front gardens (the result of a design competition organised by the *Sunday Times*); a fruit and herb garden display by Highfield Nurseries with a fruit tunnel centring on a large statue of Pomona, goddess of fruit; and Torbay Borough Council's guardsman seated on a horse in front of a sentry box, made entirely of succulent plants and herbaceous perennials.

Before his marriage, Prince Charles rarely attended Chelsea Flower Show, but now he has a home of his own at Highgrove and a wife who loves flowers (inset, top left) he takes a more active interest (main picture). Princess Alexandra (bottom left) likes to order plants for the garden of Thatched House Lodge in Richmond Park and the Queen and Princess Margaret (top, far left) have been keen gardeners since, as children, they helped their parents to restore the gardens of the Royal Lodge Windsor

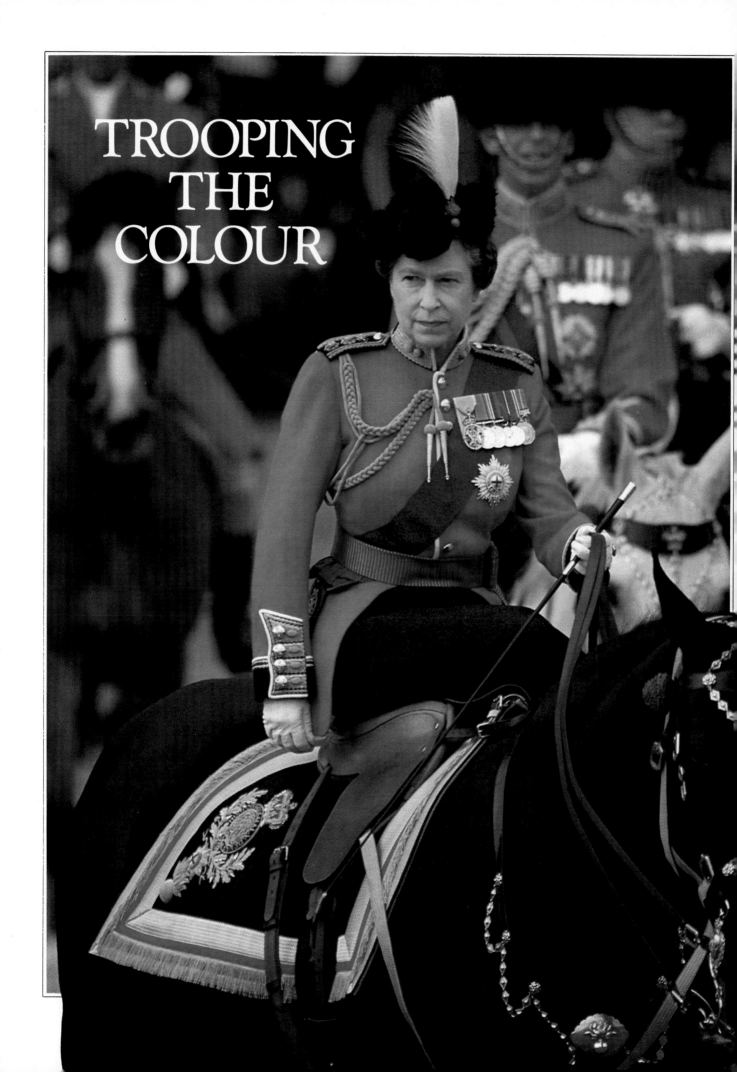

TROOPING
THE
COLOUR

One of the year's most popular events is the military pageant known as Trooping the Colour, held on the Queen's official birthday in June. Crowds flock for a sight of the Queen, in the uniform of colonel-in-chief, riding side-saddle from Buckingham Palace to Horse Guards Parade where the ceremony is held.

First recorded in 1755, the ceremony of Trooping the Colour derives from the old custom of trooping the regimental flag through the ranks every evening so that every soldier in the regiment could recognise it and rally to it on the field of battle. The last time the colours were actually carried into battle was during the Crimean War. Since 1805 the ceremony has taken place on the sovereign's official birthday (now usually the second Saturday in June). There are seven regiments (two cavalry and five regiments of Foot Guards) in the Queen's Household Division and each regiment has two colours – the sovereign's colour and the regimental colour. As colonel-in-chief, the Queen selects the regiment (one of the Foot Guards) whose colours are trooped at the birthday parade. Riding side-saddle, the Queen leads the parade wearing the scarlet tunic and hat plume of the regiment whose colour is being trooped. Here (far left) in 1984 she is wearing the white plume of the Grenadier Guards. After the opening display of counter-marching at Horse Guards Parade, the colour Escort marches to the centre of the parade ground and halts facing the colour. The regimental sergeant-major hands the heavy colour over to the colour ensign (left); the ensign then carries the colour for the rest of the ceremony. When the royal salute has been given, the Guards march back to Buckingham Palace. After the ceremony is over members of the royal family appear on the balcony of the palace to watch RAF Strike Command fly past; in 1984 Prince William made his first balcony appearance (left). Earlier, little Zara Phillips had watched the parade from a window (above)

THE WIMBLEDON FINALS

lorious weather graced the two weeks of Wimbledon in 1984. This historic tournament, first staged in 1877, provided plenty of interest for serious followers of tennis – and for thousands of others who simply wanted an enjoyable day out, seeing the 'stars' in action, sipping champagne, enjoying strawberries and cream and just catching some sun. Among the spectators was the Princess of Wales, who watched the quarter-finals match on the centre court between Chris Lloyd and Sweden's Carina Karlsson, which Mrs Lloyd won in resounding fashion. The Duke of Kent, who is president of the All England Lawn Tennis Club, and the Duchess of Kent presented the trophies and cheques to the winners on the final two days of the tournament.

Royal visitors to Wimbledon included the Princess of Wales with her sister Lady Jane Fellowes (above) and the Duchess of Kent (below). Both top singles seeds were victorious in 1984. Martina Navratilova (left, receiving her trophy from the Duchess of Kent) defeated Chris Lloyd in a thrilling match, and John McEnroe (right, after the presentation) took just 80 minutes to dispatch Jimmy Connors. McEnroe won £120,000 prize money, and Miss Navratilova £108,400

ROYAL ASCOT

A short distance from Windsor, the Royal Ascot racecourse was initially laid out in 1711 by order of Queen Anne. Since then, every reigning monarch apart from William IV has regularly attended Ascot Week in June. Notable meetings include the 2½-mile Gold Cup, first held in 1807, and the 1½-mile King George VI and Queen Elizabeth Stakes in July.

Famous for its parade of fashionable clothes and exotic millinery (inset below, Princess Michael of Kent in an extravagantly beribboned confection), Ladies' Day at Ascot is regarded as the peak of the London 'season'. On royal race days a procession of carriages led by the Queen and Prince Philip, and escorted by riders in scarlet and gold livery, proceeds along the New Mile course to the royal enclosure (main picture and inset left)

ROYAL SCOTLAND

The palace of Holyroodhouse, which was originally a guest house attached to a medieval monastery, stands at the eastern end of the Royal Mile sloping down from Edinburgh Castle. It is the Queen's official residence in Scotland. Garden parties, investitures and official State visits all take place here when the Queen is staying in Scotland. Holyroodhouse became the chief residence of the Scottish monarchs from the time that James II decided to make Edinburgh the Scottish capital in 1437. James IV of Scotland built the existing north-west tower in about 1501. It was in this tower that David Rizzio, Italian secretary of Mary Queen of Scots and suspected by the Queen's husband, Lord Darnley, of being her lover, was stabbed to death in 1566 when Mary was pregnant with the future James VI of Scotland (who was to become James I of England).

The Queen holds court at Holyroodhouse for a week each July. In 1984 she managed to carry out some 16 official engagements between 2 and 7 July.

On her arrival in Edinburgh on 2 July the Queen was, as is customary, handed the keys of the city on a red velvet cushion by the Lord Lieutenant. The Queen then inspected the Guard of Honour, a column of immaculately turned out soldiers from the Argyll and Sutherland Highlanders (left: below and inset). On the fifth day of her stay, the Queen fulfilled seven engagements in Berwickshire, ending with a visit to Eyemouth (below) where she unveiled a plaque for the Royal British Legion Housing Association and visited the Disabled Centre. The Queen seemed to enjoy the relaxed informality of these occasions

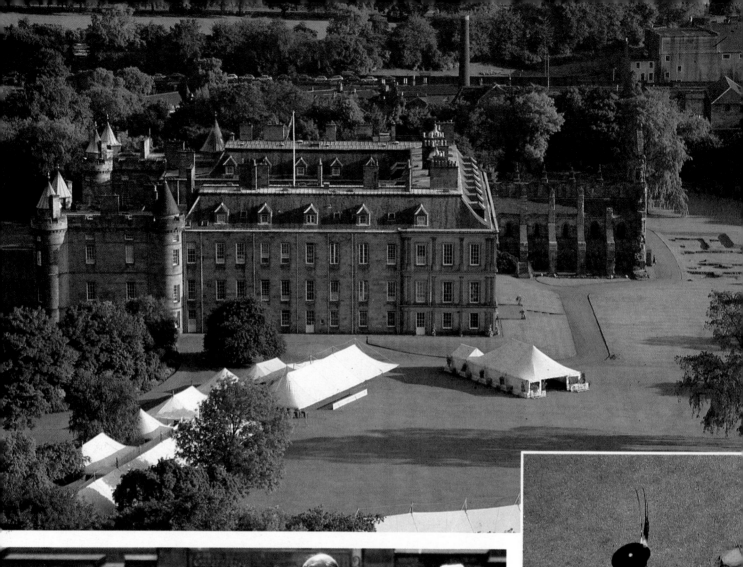

The grounds of Holyroodhouse (top) provide a rather more spectacular setting for the annual garden party than the grounds of Buckingham Palace. A select few of the 8000 guests were presented to the Queen (above) who looked elegant in an emerald silk outfit. The Order of the Thistle ceremony, one of the most picturesque royal events, took place on 2 July. The Queen, Prince Philip and the Prince of Wales were driven in the Scottish State coach (top) along the cobbled streets to St Giles's Cathedral

First, the Queen was greeted by the Lord Lieutenant, Councillor John McKay, who handed over the keys of the city in a simple ceremony. After inspecting the Guard of Honour of the Argyll and Sutherland Highlanders, the Queen attended the Ceremony of the Thistle (the Scottish equivalent of the Order of the Garter) at St Giles's Cathedral.

On 3 July the Queen attended the centenary exhibition of the Royal Scottish Geographical Society, of which she is patron, and the next day visited Queensbury House Hospital, which was celebrating its 150th anniversary. She then returned to Holyroodhouse where she gave a garden party. The Queen, Prince Philip, Princess Anne and Alice, Duchess of Gloucester, chatted to some of the 8000 guests while the band of the Argyll and Sutherland Highlanders played in the background.

The fifth day of the visit focused on Berwickshire where the Queen carried out no fewer than seven engagements, including opening a new tourist information centre and touring a complex of grain driers and stores. The week was a hectic one, but the Queen appeared to enjoy every moment.

where they were received by the minister and Lord Home, the former prime minister. Now Chancellor of the Thistle, he was admitted to the Order by the Queen in 1962. As Sovereign of the Order, the Queen, resplendent in her dark velvet robes and plumed hat (right) presided over the ceremony. On 4 July the Queen and Prince Philip visited Queensbury House Hospital, originally a shelter for the poor and now devoted mainly to geriatric cases, to honour its 150th anniversary (left)

THE QUEEN MOTHER'S BIRTHDAY

The Queen Mother's birthday on 4 August has become something of an institution. In a simple but moving ceremony, the second battalion the Grenadier Guards marches past Clarence House playing 'Happy Birthday To You' and the Queen Mother emerges to greet the crowds of well-wishers and to receive posies from children.

As old as the century, and in fine fettle after her three-day hospital check-up, the Queen Mother chased away the rain on her 84th birthday. As if on cue, as she emerged from Clarence House to greet the crowds the sun came out (below). With Prince Philip and Princess Anne in Los Angeles for the Olympic Games, the Queen Mother was joined for lunch by her favourite grandson, the Prince of Wales, who flew in from Monte Carlo, and his cousins, Viscount Linley and Lady Sarah Armstrong-Jones (left)

HOLIDAY AT BALMORAL

Balmoral is the Queen's much loved private Scottish home where she spends six weeks every summer. Here the royal family can enjoy walking and picnicking in the glorious Scottish countryside, or spend a day quietly fishing for salmon in the river Dee. Like Sandringham, Balmoral is a place where the Queen and her family can dispense with much of the formality that normally surrounds them.

It was Prince Albert who first acquired a lease of Balmoral in 1848, after he and Queen Victoria had fallen in love with the Scottish Highlands. The existing castle, which had been extensively altered in the 1830s, was a strange mixture of Jacobean windows, Tudor chimneys and defensive parapets. The architect, John Smith (nicknamed 'Tudor Johnnie') from Aberdeen, had completely transformed the old building, leaving only the 17th-century tower untouched. He also added a conservatory, so starting a fashion.

This castle, however, soon proved to be too small for the royal couple, their children, staff and guests, and Prince Albert commissioned a new enlarged Balmoral to be built in the romantic Scottish baronial style. The new building, with its pointed turrets and towers, set in the wild scenery, reminded the Prince of the scenes of his early childhood in Germany.

From the first, Victoria and Albert's way of life at Balmoral was extremely informal. In 1849 the prime minister, Lord John Russell, wrote of the Queen's new Highland retreat:

> The place is very pretty, the house very small. . . . They live with the greatest simplicity and ease. He shoots every morning, returns to luncheon, and then they walk or drive. She is running in and out of the house all day long, and often goes about alone, walks into cottages, sits down and chats with the old women . . .

The betrothal of the Princess Royal to Prince Frederick William of Prussia took place at Balmoral in 1855, and Florence Nightingale was invited there to discuss the problems of the Army in the Crimea.

In the uncertain years immediately after the First World War, Balmoral's unbroken links with the past were a source of strength to George V. Faced with a socialist government, he felt it 'ought to be treated fairly' and he invited the prime minister Ramsay MacDonald to Balmoral, where the King went every autumn to shoot game on the estate. The tradition of entertaining prime ministers there was continued by George VI and, in 1938, when Neville Chamberlain was staying there, the young Princesses Elizabeth and Margaret persuaded him to slide down a steep grass terrace on a tea-tray.

The present royal family now 'escape' to Balmoral every year during August and September.

Famous for the Changing of the Guard ceremony that takes place on most mornings throughout the year (above), Buckingham Palace is a 'must' with tourists. The Queen's favourite room is the White Drawing Room (bottom, far left) where she receives new ambassadors and where guests assemble before a State function such as a banquet or ball. The 12 sculptured panels over the frieze and cornice depicting children at play were designed in 1831 by the artist William Pitts. There is apparently no door to the suite of State Apartments beyond the White Drawing Room; access is via a huge mirror in one wall that swings open to reveal a vista of great splendour: the lofty oval Music Room leading to the Blue Drawing Room, which gives on to the State Dining Room (hung with Gainsborough's portraits of the Queen's ancestors), the West Gallery and, at the end of this impressive suite of State Apartments designed by John Nash for George IV, the magnificent Ballroom, 123 feet (37 metres) long, which was added to the south wing of the palace in 1854. At one end are two stately thrones set under a canopy (top left) formed from the awning beneath which George V and Queen Mary sat at the Delhi Durbar in 1911. At the other end of the Ballroom stands the great organ and musicians' gallery. This room is used for State banquets and investitures as well as State balls. The guest rooms (left, an example) are to be found on the second or 'bedroom' floor

On the day of the State Opening of
Parliament the Queen drives down the
Mall (left) from Buckingham Palace in
the Irish State Coach and arrives at
Westminster at 11 a.m. (above)

THE STATE OPENING OF PARLIAMENT

The State Opening of Parliament – held annually in October or November – is one of the most magnificent royal ceremonies of the year. It carries many reminders of the centuries of history that have resulted in the style of democracy we have today. 'Parliament' derives from the Norman French word for 'talk'; the first 'parlement' was introduced by William the Conqueror who would summon a group of barons to his court about three times a year to consult with him about affairs of government.

On the day of the State Opening of Parliament, the Queen drives in procession from Buckingham Palace to the Houses of Parliament; there, in the robing room, she puts on the Imperial State Crown and the 18-feet (5.5 metre) long crimson Robe of State. Escorted by Prince Philip, the Queen then proceeds to her throne in the House of Lords, where the Lord Chancellor presents her with the 'Gracious Speech'. Before she reads the speech, representatives of the Commons are summoned. Because Charles I violated the privilege of the Commons, the sovereign is not allowed to enter the lower chamber. So the Lord Great Chamberlain dispatches Black Rod to the Commons – where, symbolically, the door is first slammed in his face by a Serjeant-at-Arms. Black Rod then knocks three times, and summons the Commons to attend the Queen in the upper chamber. The Queen then reads the 'Gracious Speech', which contains the proposals of 'her' Government for the coming year.

At the Royal Entrance (top left) the Queen and Prince Philip are greeted by the Earl Marshal of England and the Lord Great Chamberlain to a fanfare of trumpets. The royal regalia (brought from the Tower of London) travel in a coach of their own (above); regalia used at the State Opening include the Imperial State Crown, the Cap of Maintenance and the Sword of State

THE CENOTAPH CEREMONY

The Queen leads the nation in honouring the memory of the war dead at the Cenotaph (above). The medals and poppies worn by ex-servicemen and the plumes of the Household Cavalry bring touches of colour to the scene (below)

O n Remembrance Sunday – the second Sunday in November – the nation pays homage to those who died in battle for Great Britain, the Empire and Commonwealth. Although it is an act of remembrance for all war dead, the service – which is distinguished by its simplicity – especially recalls those who died in the First and Second World Wars. The dignified and moving ceremony is relayed 'live' on TV and radio.

The Cenotaph, which forms the focal point of the service, was erected in London's Whitehall to honour the dead of the First World War. It bears the inscription 'The Glorious Dead'. Here in Whitehall each November the service of remembrance is performed 'lest we forget'.

As massed regimental bands play appropriately sombre music, units of the Army, Navy and Air Force take up their allotted positions in the area surrounding the Cenotaph. They are joined by veterans of the two world wars and those who have seen active service in areas such as Northern Ireland and the Falklands. The general public are placed further back and hear the service via loudspeakers, which are specially rigged up for the occasion.

The Queen's arrival is timed to coincide with the striking of the 11th hour by Big Ben. At this moment, too, a gun salute is fired. As the boom subsides it ushers in two minutes of silence. At the end of this interval another salute is fired and the Last Post is played.

Wreaths are then laid at the base of the Cenotaph. The Queen is the first to step forward and is followed by other members of the royal family. Leaders of the main political parties come next, headed by the prime minister, followed by representatives of Commonwealth countries, the diplomatic corps and the armed forces. After the wreaths have been placed the Bishop of London conducts a brief service, at the conclusion of which the Reveille is sounded. This is followed by the playing of the national anthem. The Queen then leaves, as do the officials. The proceedings are brought to an end as the veterans march past the Cenotaph to the strains of popular wartime tunes.

Bandsmen march in procession to the Cenotaph watched by members of the public several lines deep (above). For the Queen and the royal family the annual service of remembrance is a moving occasion (below)

CHRISTMAS AT WINDSOR CASTLE

The delightful and secluded moat garden
(left), made in the dry moat of the castle,
is overlooked by the Devil's Tower
where, in the early 15th century, the
young James I of Scotland was
imprisoned for several years. The
imposing gallery and banqueting
chamber (right), named the Waterloo
Chamber, was built by George IV to
commemorate the defeat of Napoleon by
the allied forces at the battle of
Waterloo in 1815. The room is hung with
portraits of the kings, politicians and
generals who played a part in the
successful campaign, with the Duke of
Wellington in pride of place

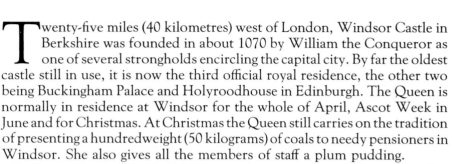

Twenty-five miles (40 kilometres) west of London, Windsor Castle in Berkshire was founded in about 1070 by William the Conqueror as one of several strongholds encircling the capital city. By far the oldest castle still in use, it is now the third official royal residence, the other two being Buckingham Palace and Holyroodhouse in Edinburgh. The Queen is normally in residence at Windsor for the whole of April, Ascot Week in June and for Christmas. At Christmas the Queen still carries on the tradition of presenting a hundredweight (50 kilograms) of coals to needy pensioners in Windsor. She also gives all the members of staff a plum pudding.

In Henry II's reign (1154–1189) the castle was transformed from a wooden fortress into a more permanent stone building with living quarters and gardens. Edward III was born at Windsor and celebrated his victories over the Scots and French by founding in 1348 England's leading Order of Chivalry, the Order of the Garter. The name of this Order is said to have arisen from the garter dropped at a ball by the Countess of Salisbury, a celebrated beauty. When the King retrieved it, some of the courtiers took it as an amorous gesture, leading the King to pronounce the words, '*Honi soit qui mal y pense*' ('Shame on him who thinks ill of it'), adding that the garter would be advanced to so high an honour that they would be happy to wear it themselves. And so it was to be.

The Chapel of St George – started in Henry II's reign – still forms the setting for the Service of the Garter, normally held each year on the Monday in Ascot Week (the ceremony was not held in 1984).

Windsor Castle is divided into three wards – Lower, Middle and Upper. The main gateway, built by Henry VIII in 1509, leads into the Lower Ward that houses St George's Chapel, the Albert Memorial Chapel, the lodgings of the Military Knights of Windsor and the Round Tower built by Henry II in the 12th century as the castle's main stronghold. Access to the Upper Ward is via the Norman Gate (it is in fact 14th century) and immediately beyond this are the buildings that house the royal library. Here visitors may buy tickets to see the State Apartments in the Upper Ward, Queen Mary's Dolls' House and the exhibition of drawings by Leonardo da Vinci, Holbein and others. The Queen's private apartments are also in the Upper Ward.

Part IV
A FAMILY AT WORK

Many of the day-to-day engagements of the royal family go unrecorded in the national Press. While the spectacular events such as Trooping the Colour and the State Opening of Parliament receive top media coverage, the daily royal round of visits, openings and inspections may only get noticed locally. Yet it is this very presence of royalty at grassroots level – inspecting a factory or hospital, or launching a ship – that does much to validate the efforts of ordinary people. And it is these constant bread-and-butter duties – the royal family's 'work' – that in the eyes of many people justify the expense of the monarchy, while the opportunity to meet the Queen or shake the Princess of Wales by the hand does much to sustain the enormous popularity that the royal family currently enjoys.

It was the grandmother of the family who led by example in terms of unflagging professionalism during 1984. The Queen Mother carried out well over 100 engagements, all with her customary sparkle and charm. She is commander-in-chief of 18 regiments and patron of more than 300 bodies, and she took on yet more responsibilities with the presidency of the Victoria Cross and George Cross Association. The Queen undertook the greatest number of engagements during the year. Her two weeks in Canada in the autumn were probably the most taxing – a crammed 15 days of toing and froing across the countryside. Afterwards she enjoyed a well-earned rest in the horse-breeding centre of Kentucky. In 1984 Prince Philip was much involved with his work for the World Wildlife Fund and a new collection of his writing – *Men, Machines and Sacred Cows* – was published in February.

Following the birth of Prince Henry the Prince and Princess of Wales chose to spend as much time as possible with their children. But prior to the birth they had both made regular public appearances. Charles travelled widely both at home and abroad, and still found time to make some outspoken pronouncements on the state of modern architecture and on health. Princess Anne carried out the second highest number of engagements during the year, winning admiration for her efforts both at home and overseas on behalf of the Save the Children Fund. In 1984 Prince Andrew was 'blooded' as a member of the royal touring team before resuming his life as a naval officer. He also made his début as a photographer by taking the pictures for the 1985 Ilford calendar. Prince Edward continued to enjoy college life to the full at Cambridge, as well as learning to fly and training to become a marine.

In the 'second team' Princess Margaret worked strenuously on behalf of a range of children's associations while the Duke and Duchess of Kent carried out many engagements connected with their own interests of sport and music. The Duke and Duchess of Gloucester, Princess Alexandra and Prince and Princess Michael of Kent all had busy schedules. Everyone played their part with enthusiasm and grace.

During 1984 the Queen undertook more
engagements than any other member of
the royal family. As well as travelling
thousands of miles to make visits to
Jordan and Canada, she made the short
day trip across the channel to Normandy
for the D-Day celebrations in France. At
home she carried out literally hundreds
of duties all over the country. In May,
for instance, in the space of six days, she
opened the International Garden Festival
in Liverpool and the Thames flood
barrier in London. The pressures of the
Queen's official and public life (left,
arriving back from Scotland in July)
make the moments of relaxation and
family life particularly precious;
whenever possible the Queen's corgis
accompany her on her travels (inset, one
of the royal corgis with its handler on
the return from Scotland). The Queen
was delighted with the birth in
September of her fourth grandchild,
Prince Henry, to the Prince and Princess
of Wales (bottom left). Both Charles and
Diana displayed a new confidence during
the year, with the Prince making an
innovatory appearance on the BBC
children's television programme,
Jackanory, reading the story he
originally wrote for his two younger
brothers, *The Old Man of Lochnagar*.
The Queen Mother (above, leaving the
Sandringham Flower Show in June)
continued to be as energetic as ever. Her
tour of the Channel Islands on the royal
yacht *Britannia* in the early summer was
a great success; she was greeted by
enthusiastic crowds at every stop, and
revealed a previously hidden talent –
playing pool

DIARY OF EVENTS

The following are just a few of the many engagements, both at home and abroad, that the royal family carried out during 1984

January
10 Duchess of Kent visits Institute for the Blind, Norwich
23–27 Princess Anne visits USA to support fund-raising activities of British Olympic Association

February
6 Prince Philip launches Norfolk Outward Bound Association at King's Lynn
7–8 Prince Philip visits University of Cambridge
11 Princess of Wales attends gala performance of *Carmen* by London City Ballet in Oslo
11–15 Princess Anne attends Winter Olympics at Sarajevo, Yugoslavia
14–16 Prince Philip attends meetings of World Wildlife Fund in Switzerland
15 Duchess of Gloucester attends fashion and music evening in aid of Asthma Society
15 Duke of Kent visits University of Surrey, Guildford
15–25 Princess Anne visits Morocco, The Gambia and Upper Volta
17 Prince Philip visits Dutch HQ of World Wildlife Fund, Zeist
21 Prince Philip attends luncheon on publication of his book *Men, Machines and Sacred Cows*
22 Princess of Wales visits national HQ of British Red Cross Youth, London
23 Queen and Prince Philip give lunch for President of Italy
23 Prince of Wales attends independence celebrations, Brunei
23 Queen Mother attends concert in Westminster Abbey to mark 50th anniversary of death of Elgar
23 Princess Alexandra names new lifeboat at Cowes
28 Duchess of Gloucester visits HQ of Royal Army Educational Corps at Eltham, London
29 Prince and Princess of Wales attend Genesis concert in Solihull

March
1 Princess Alice, Duchess of Gloucester, visits RAF Swinderby, Lincolnshire
4 Princess Anne attends Children's Royal Variety Performance in London in aid of National Society for the Prevention of Cruelty to Children
8 Princess Anne visits British School of Osteopathy, London
9 Prince Philip delivers Chancellor's lecture, Edinburgh University

12 Queen and Prince Philip attend Commonwealth Day service at Westminster Abbey
13 Princess of Wales visits the rheumatology unit, Hammersmith Hospital, London
14 Duchess of Gloucester opens St John Ambulance Museum, London
15 Princess Anne presents trophy to leading jockey at Cheltenham races
17 Queen Mother presents shamrock to 1st Battalion the Irish Guards at Münster, West Germany
17 Princess Anne attends National Shire Horse Show, Peterborough
19 Princess Anne opens Portland Hospital for Women and Children, London
19 (until 3 April) Prince of Wales visits Tanzania, Zambia, Botswana and Zimbabwe as member of Board of Commonwealth Development Corporation
21 Queen and Prince Philip give reception for winners of Queen's Awards for Export and Technology
22 Princess Margaret attends ceremony at Chelmsford Cathedral on completion of restoration work
23 Princess of Wales opens spinal injuries unit at branch of Royal National Orthopaedic Hospital, Stanmore
25 Princess Anne presents awards at British Academy of Film and Television Arts
25 Queen Mother attends final of Milk Cup at Wembley
26–30 Queen and Prince Philip pay State visit to Jordan
28 Queen Mother unveils memorial to Noel Coward in Westminster Abbey
29 Princess Anne attends reception at 10 Downing Street for British Olympics team
30 Princess Alexandra attends Royal Air Force Anniversary Concert, London

April
1–10 Prince Andrew visits St Helena for 150th anniversary celebrations of Crown colony status
5 Queen Mother opens Leukaemia Research Laboratories at University College Hospital, London
6 Queen and Prince Philip visit the Queen's Flight at RAF Benson, Oxfordshire
6 Duchess of Kent takes salute at Sovereign's Parade, Royal Military Academy, Sandhurst
10–13 Queen and Prince Philip are hosts to Emir of Bahrain
14–15 Queen attends Badminton Horse Trials, Gloucestershire
15–20 Prince Andrew visits Los Angeles for official engagements

17 Princess Alexandra attends celebrity awards of Television and Radio Industries Club
18 Queen and Prince Philip visit King Edward VII Hospital, Windsor
27 Princess Anne dines with Students' Association at London University

May
1 Prince Philip presents Design Council Awards at RAF Museum, Hendon
2 Queen opens International Garden Festival at Liverpool
2–4 Prince Philip visits Vienna for World Wildlife Fund functions
3 Prince Andrew opens *The Lives of the Saints* photographic exhibition in London
3 Princess Margaret opens Parkinson's Disease research centre, Denmark Hill, London
4 Queen Mother attends Silver Jubilee celebrations of De Havilland Aircraft Museum Trust at Hatfield
8 Queen opens Thames flood barrier
8 Princess of Wales receives Honorary Fellowship of Royal College of Physicians and Surgeons, Glasgow
10 Duke of Kent visits lifeboat stations, Orkney Islands
10 Duchess of Kent opens new wing at Leeds General Infirmary
15 Queen Mother presents Royal National Lifeboat Institution awards in London
15 Princess Margaret attends Wedgwood exhibition to mark firm's 225th anniversary
16 Queen and Prince Philip visit Emmanuel and Jesus Colleges, Cambridge
16 Prince Michael of Kent opens Institute of Motor Industry conference at Heathrow
16–17 Duchess of Kent visits British units in West Germany
17 Prince of Wales visits Jorvik Viking centre and Coppergate Development, York
19 Duke and Duchess of Kent attend FA Cup final at Wembley
20 Duke of Kent unveils Fred Perry Gates and statue at Wimbledon
20–22 Prince Philip visits Washington, DC, for World Wildlife Fund meetings
22 Princess Margaret attends AGM of Girl Guides Association
22–25 Queen visits Royal Regiment of Artillery and Royal Green Jackets in West Germany
23 Duchess of Kent hosts 21st anniversary concert of Yehudi Menuhin School at St James's Palace
24 Duke of Kent chairs AGM of Automobile Association in London
24 Queen Mother opens Maritime Museum in Aberdeen
30 Queen opens new terminal at Birmingham airport and visits *Expo 84* exhibition

30 Prince and Princess of Wales visit Chester
30 Prince of Wales addresses Royal Institute of British Architects at Hampton Court Palace
30 (to 1 June) Queen Mother visits Channel Islands

June
2 Prince and Princess of Wales attend dinner in aid of United World Colleges and Mary Rose Trust, Surrey
2 Prince Michael of Kent presents Royal Lifesaving Society Awards in London
3 Queen Mother attends D-Day service at Portsmouth Cathedral and opens city's D-Day Museum
4 Princess Alexandra opens Maidstone Hospital, Kent
5 Prince of Wales attends D-Day anniversary ceremony at Ranville, France
6 Queen and Prince Philip attend ceremonies marking 40th anniversary of the D-Day landings in France
8 Queen visits South of England Show at Ardingly
8 Prince Philip presents new colours to 1st Battalion the Duke of Edinburgh's Royal Regiment (Berkshire and Wiltshire) at Canterbury
8 Princess Anne takes Queen's Review at RAF College Cranwell, Lincolnshire
8 Princess Alice, Duchess of Gloucester, visits 1st Battalion the King's Own Scottish Borderers at Colchester
9 Queen and Prince Philip give dinner for Heads of State and delegation leaders attending economic summit
11 Princess Anne opens new library at Exeter University
13 Prince of Wales visits Cranfield Institute of Technology, Bedford
14 Prince Philip confers honorary degrees at Cambridge
14 Queen visits HQ of British Council to mark its jubilee and later witnesses the ceremony of Beating Retreat, Prince Philip taking the salute
14 Princess Anne attends Royal International Horse Show, Birmingham
14–21 Princess Alexandra visits USA, attending gala performances by the English National Opera in New Orleans and New York
17 Duchess of Gloucester presents trophies to winners at Stella Artois Lawn Tennis championships, London
21 Prince of Wales opens library extension at St David's University College, Lampeter
22 Princess Anne opens new wing at YMCA, Bournemouth
24 Prince Andrew presents prizes at British Helicopter Championships, Northamptonshire
27 Prince of Wales opens Duke of Cornwall Spinal Treatment Centre, Odstock Hospital, Salisbury

July
3 Queen and Prince Philip attend Service of Installation of the Knights of the Thistle, Edinburgh
3 Princess Margaret attends degree conferment ceremony, Keele University
3–4 Duke of Kent visits Royal Show at Stoneleigh, Warwickshire
4 Queen and Prince Philip host garden party at Holyroodhouse, Edinburgh
4 Duke of Gloucester attends AGM of Cancer Research Campaign
4 Princess Alexandra attends the Anglo-American Ball in London
7–9 Princess Anne attends opening of Royal Opera season, Los Angeles
9 Prince of Wales opens *Mary Rose* Exhibition at Portsmouth
9–11 Princess Alexandra presides at degree ceremonies, Lancaster University
11 Prince Philip attends service marking completion of first half of Westminster Abbey restoration work
11 Prince of Wales visits British servicemen at Laarbruch, West Germany
11 Princess Margaret opens exhibition of *Treasures from St Mark's Cathedral, Venice,* at British Museum
11 Prince Michael of Kent takes salute at Royal Tournament, London
11–13 Princess Anne visits Atlanta, Georgia, to support fund-raising efforts of British Olympic Association
12 Queen, with Duke and Duchess of Kent, attends Service of the Order of St Michael and St George in St Paul's Cathedral
13 Duke of Gloucester enrolled as a Senior Fellow at Royal College of Art
13 Duke of Kent presides at degree ceremony, University of Surrey
14 Prince Michael of Kent starts Round Britain Offshore Power Boat Race at Portsmouth
16 Prince Philip presents new Colours to 2nd Battalion Royal Canadian Regiment at Gagetown, New Brunswick, Canada
19 Prince of Wales attends conference on conventional and complementary medicine, London
19–20 Duchess of Kent presides at degree ceremonies, University of Leeds
22 Prince Michael of Kent attends British Grand Prix at Brands Hatch
24 Prince Andrew takes salute at Royal Tournament, London
26 Princess Alexandra attends final night of Carl Flesch Violin Competition and presents prizes
27 (to 12 August) Prince Philip and Princess Anne attend Olympic Games in Los Angeles
31 Queen attends Glyndebourne Opera in honour of company's Golden Jubilee

August
2 Queen leaves Southampton in *Britannia* for cruise to Aberdeen via Western Isles

6–10 Prince of Wales visits Papua New Guinea and opens new Parliament building
27 Princess Anne attends Greater London Horse Show
31 Princess Anne installed as president of the Missions to Seamen

September
4 Prince Michael of Kent attends Farnborough air show
15 Princess Margaret attends concert in Glasgow in aid of Royal Scottish Society for the Prevention of Cruelty to Children
17 Princess Anne attends Frank Sinatra concert in aid of Order of St John
22 Princess Alexandra attends World Ploughing Championships at Wispington, Lincolnshire
23 Prince of Wales attends service at Oosterbeek war cemetery, Holland, to mark 40th anniversary of Battle of Arnhem
24 (to 7 October) Queen and Prince Philip visit Canada
25 Princess Alexandra opens national exhibition of children's art, London
26 Princess Anne installed as Master of Worshipful Company of Farriers
28 Queen Mother opens Commonwealth Parliamentary Association conference in Isle of Man

October
1–3 Princess Anne visits Isle of Man
4–6 Princess Anne visits Jersey to attend 21st anniversary celebrations of Jersey Wildlife Preservation Trust
8–15 Queen pays private visit to USA
11 Princess Anne visits British School, The Hague
15 Princess Anne opens Avon Riding Centre for the Disabled, Bristol
23 The Queen hosts State banquet at Buckingham Palace for President Mitterrand of France
23 (to 4 November) Princess Anne travels to Bangladesh and India as President of the Save the Children Fund

November
7 Queen attends service at St Paul's to mark centenary of National Society for the Prevention of Cruelty to Children
14 Queen and Prince Philip attend dinner given by Commonwealth High Commissioners
19 Queen Mother attends Royal Variety Performance, London
20 Princess Anne attends Variety Club of Great Britain's Women of the Year Awards, Leeds

December
6 Princess Anne attends awards dinner of Sports Writers' Association in London
20 Queen and Prince Philip attend gala performance of *The Nutcracker* at Royal Opera House in aid of the NSPCC

THE QUEEN

For the Queen, 1984 contained some memorable major engagements that punctuated a typically crowded year of official duties, receptions and occasions of purely private pleasure. Her overseas tours were more demanding than usual. In March the five-day State visit to Jordan, a country embroiled in the turbulent politics of the Middle East, was surrounded by the most elaborate security precautions ever taken for any visit by the Queen. For the D-Day anniversary celebrations in Normandy on 6 June the Queen, who has an intense dislike of helicopter travel, was compelled by her schedule to be whisked to four separate services in the course of seven hours.

The two-week tour of Canada, postponed from July because of elections, went ahead in September and took the Queen and Prince Philip to New Brunswick, Ontario and Manitoba. At its conclusion the Queen, a horse-breeder of international repute, was able to relax on a week's private visit to Kentucky. There she was shown around notable stud farms and was able to assess top stallions at her leisure.

At home the International Garden Festival in Liverpool provided one of the most enjoyable occasions of the year, and in her speech at the opening on 2 May the Queen remarked: 'The gardens and exhibitions blooming on this site are

The Queen's official round is enlivened by less formal occasions – yet no matter where she is in public the Queen is always on show (opposite, enjoying a walkabout in Scotland). In March 1984 the Queen and Prince Philip attended a gala performance of the Andrew Lloyd Webber musical *Starlight Express* and met the composer (right, above). When free of official engagements the Queen derives great pleasure from watching polo (centre right, enjoying a chat with two referees) and is also an enthusiastic photographer (right, at the Royal Windsor Horse Show)

The Queen's official engagements range all over the country and involve meeting people from all walks of life. At the International Garden Festival in Liverpool the Queen found much to interest and delight her. The architectural formality of the Italian exhibit (above) was in marked contrast to the design of the Canadian garden, which featured a specially carved totem pole 12 feet (3.5 metres) high (left). At the Sandringham Flower Show the Queen was entertained by territorial soldiers (top right) and in Hackney, London, she met patients at St Joseph's Hospice (right, centre). In May she opened the Thames flood barrier; behind the official party (right) are two of the massive gates that can close in 30 minutes to shut out a surge tide

symbolic of what we all wish for Liverpool.' Created from 250 acres (101 hectares) of derelict dockland, the gardens included thematic displays and exhibitions.

Six days later there was another occasion of major significance, only this time nearer 'home'. On the afternoon of 8 May the Queen formally opened the Thames flood barrier, 10 massive steel and concrete structures spanning the river at Woolwich. Designed to save London from flooding by surge tides, it forms one of the most impressive engineering feats in the world.

If these were among the formal highlights of her year, the many private, personal occasions were, as ever, greatly cherished by the Queen. The weekends spent at Windsor, watching Charles play polo or enjoying the company of her grandchildren; the retreats to Sandringham and Balmoral for holidays and family get-togethers; the pleasure of Royal Ascot week in June; the delight in the birth of Prince Henry – these simple, domestic occasions assume a very special importance for a monarch as hardworking as the Queen.

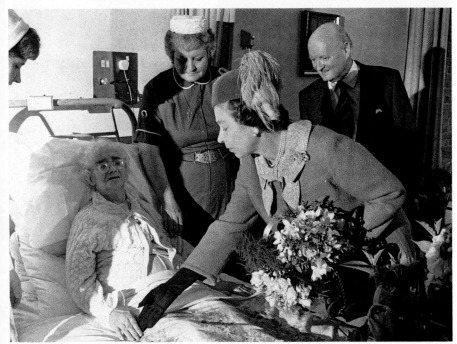

PRINCE PHILIP

Energetic and forthright, Prince Philip manages for most of the time to get the balance right in his difficult role as royal consort in a swiftly changing world. Throughout 1984 he carried out his duties in a typically robust fashion.

He accompanied the Queen on her highly publicised State visit to Jordan and on the two-week tour of Canada later in the year. In June he went with her to the D-Day celebrations in France, and his duties as president of the World Wildlife Fund International took him to Switzerland, West Germany and Holland in February and Austria and the United States in May. He also attended the Olympic Games in Los Angeles in his capacity as president of the International Equestrian Federation.

At home his schedule included several receptions for young people who had reached the Gold Standard in the Duke of Edinburgh's Award Scheme, and as Chancellor of the University of Cambridge he was required to fulfil engagements in the city in February and June.

February also saw the publication of his latest book, *Men, Machines and Sacred Cows*, which is a characteristic mixture of outspokenness and practical common sense.

Events involving horses and the armed forces loom large in Prince Philip's diary. He is a skilled carriage driver and came seventh in the Harrods International Driving Grand Prix at Windsor in May. In June he attended the Windsor Horse Trials (opposite) and Ascot, during which he watched a donkey parade (top left). On 14 June, as captain-general of the Royal Marines, he was present at the ceremony of Beating Retreat by the massed bands of the Royal Marines (left) – an impressive display of marching and countermarching held on Horse Guards Parade

123

THE PRINCE OF WALES

In an exciting year that saw the birth of his second son, the Prince of Wales continued to pursue a hectic itinerary. Apart from a flying visit to Normandy as part of the D-Day celebrations, he made several other foreign trips abroad – to Brunei in February, East Africa in March (to inspect projects run by the Commonwealth Development Corporation), Papua New Guinea in August and the Netherlands in September, to attend a ceremony to commemorate the 40th anniversary of the battle of Arnhem. Many of his engagements at home were connected with his position as president of the Prince's Trust; it was in this capacity that he attended, with the Princess of Wales, the Genesis concert in Birmingham in February and the première of the film *Indiana Jones and the Temple of Doom* in June.

Charles's interest in archaeology and the past was reflected in several of his engagements. In May he opened a new archaeology gallery in Cambridge University's Museum of Archaeology and Anthropology. The same month, as patron of the York Archaeological Trust, he opened the Jorvik Viking Centre in York. And in July he opened an exhibition in Portsmouth of artefacts recovered from the *Mary Rose*, the flagship of Henry VIII.

Shortly after the announcement of Diana's second pregnancy, Charles visited the Jaguar factory in Coventry (top). During the visit he complimented a worker on how well the production line was doing. 'Yours is doing all right too, mate,' came the reply, to gales of laughter. In March, as president, the Prince of Wales attended the Royal Naval Film Corporation's annual general meeting on board HMS *President* at King's Reach (left). In a very different guise he appeared (opposite page) on the children's BBC television programme, *Jackanory,* in September reading his own story *The Old Man of Lochnagar*

In June Prince Charles attended the memorial service in Westminster Abbey for the late Sir John Betjeman, the poet laureate, and read the first lesson.

Prince Charles has always made it plain that he is no mere figurehead, and 1984 was memorable for the forthrightness with which he expressed himself on several subjects. In May he sparked off a major row in the architectural profession by making a speech, at a dinner to mark the 150th anniversary of the Royal Institute of British Architects, attacking the whole trend of modern architecture. His outspokenness in support of holistic and alternative medicine had already, in 1983, electrified the orthodox medical profession and galvanised the British Medical Association into setting up an enquiry into alternative medical practices such as homeopathy and acupuncture; throughout 1984 Prince Charles's interest and support for complementary medical therapies was obviously growing. In an interview he confessed, 'I've always wished that I could heal,' and he revealed that he was fascinated by the relationship between mind and body, and by the power of the mind in curing illness. He stressed that 'there is a great need to be more open-minded and to admit there is more to life than meets the eye.'

This interesting heir to the throne will no doubt bring up his young sons to be unusually aware and caring Princes. It also seems likely that Prince Charles will continue to develop his own personal philosophy of life, and will keep his public guessing as to what he will do or say next.

Early in 1984 Prince Andrew gained promotion from sub-lieutenant to full lieutenant in the Royal Navy. After undertaking a training course at Portland, Dorset, he was appointed pilot of the Lynx anti-submarine helicopter of the frigate HMS *Brazen* (opposite). Despite his naval commitments he made a point of coming home for the Royal Windsor Horse Show in May (above left), an annual occasion of royal reunion. Two months later he took part in a celebrity clay pigeon shooting contest in Wales for the Save the Children Fund (left, watching others compete – and looking as if he was feeling the cold). In September the Prince was accorded the honour of his own photographic show, which was held at the Barbican Centre in London and was open to the public for more than a month. Andrew cut a dashing figure at the opening (above), which was held the same day that he had seen his youngest nephew, Prince Henry, for the first time. The basis of the exhibition was the collection of photographs that Prince Andrew had taken for the 1985 Ilford calendar

PRINCE EDWARD

During his second year at Jesus College, Cambridge, Prince Edward continued to make his mark on student life, winning over many sceptics with his shy charm and eagerness to join in activities. His exploits for the Jesus second rugby XV had to be postponed for a term – he also missed a team tour to the USA – after he contracted glandular fever early in January, but he followed up his 1983 acting début in an undergraduate production of *The Crucible* by directing a number of sketches for a summer revue.

Although he readily admits he is not the most academic student (he is reading anthropology and archaeology), Prince Edward is conscientious and enjoys any aspect of field work, like the visit he made with fellow undergraduates in August for an archaeological dig on the site of the Roman city of Wroxeter in Shropshire. At the moment, Edward is undecided as to what path he will take after obtaining his degree, but it is thought likely that he will be free to pursue a career of his own choosing.

He has one commitment on finishing his course: a year with the Royal Marines, earning his Green Beret as an officer. During the University's 1984 summer vacation, he continued his training as a cadet (begun in 1982) when he attended a two-week course at the commando HQ at Lympstone in Devon. The Prince, a second lieutenant, survived a gruelling schedule of forced marches – with an 85-lb (38.5-kilogram) back pack – long distance runs, canoeing, climbing and learning to lead patrols, and emerged to glowing reports. 'He's very good material,' one officer said. The 'baby' of the family is growing up fast.

Like any other undergraduate Prince Edward was happy to show his parents around when they came up to Cambridge in February (below). But on this occasion the Queen and Prince Philip (who is Chancellor of the University) were there to attend a dinner to mark the 400th anniversary of the Cambridge University Press at St John's College. Edward did take time off from undergraduate life, however, to attend a charity event at Ascot racecourse in June (left) – where he won a pink teddy bear

Prince Edward joins in college life to the full: acting, playing rugby and enjoying the round of social activities. During the annual University Rag Week he was asked to act as official starter to the bedstead race (left), when students in fancy dress rush through the town collecting money for charity. Although accompanied everywhere by his private detective, he tries to live as normally as possible – he is often found in the college laundrette doing his weekly wash

Edward was reminded of earlier academic days when he agreed to participate in a BBC TV programme, screened in August, on his old school, Gordonstoun (left, being interviewed by Julian Pettifer). Andrew also appeared in the film – Charles did not take part, allegedly because he hated his time at the school. During the programme Edward expounded his views on how to be a success in life: 'You don't need to have hundreds of qualifications. If you have a good personality and determination you will get there in the end'

PRINCESS ANNE

Although her official duties keep her very busy, Princess Anne still finds time for riding. She took part in the Cookham Horse Trials (far left) in March and the Windsor Horse Trials in May (above, with Zara and Peter). As colonel-in-chief of the Combined Cavalry Old Comrades, Anne attended their parade in Hyde Park (above left). The first day of July saw Princess Anne acting as her husband's loader at the celebrity clay pigeon shoot in North Wales organised by former world racing driver Jackie Stewart in aid of the Save the Children Fund (left): the winning team consisted of Captain Mark Phillips, Prince Andrew, the Duke of Kent and ex-King Constantine of Greece. September was a particularly busy month for Anne and Mark who organised horse trials to take place in the grounds of their home, Gatcombe Park

Princess Anne, who spent years at loggerheads with the media, has now become one of the most popular members of the royal family. Voted a 'sweetie' (as opposed to a 'meanie') by the *Sunday Times* in 1984, she is universally admired for her hard work on behalf of the Save the Children Fund, of which she is president.

Princess Anne has had a difficult time. While she has always been in the public eye, her importance in royal terms is constantly diminishing. From being second in line to the throne, she is now sixth, coming after her younger brothers and her two nephews, William and Henry.

In the early 1970s, when she was competing regularly in equestrian events and getting to know Captain Mark Phillips, Anne felt that the media not only failed to respect her privacy, but actually jeopardised her competitive horse-riding career by 'crowding' her.

However, today Princess Anne is one of the hardest working members of the royal 'team'. In her middle thirties she is Chancellor of London University as well as being patron or president of many organisations including the British Olympic Appeal Fund; she is also colonel-in-chief of various military units and president of the Save the Children Fund. Only the Queen carries out more official functions than Princess Anne. In 1984 Anne's trips abroad, for instance, included two visits to the United States in her capacity as president of the British Olympic Association to support fund-raising activities (plus the Olympic Games themselves in Los Angeles) and a visit to Morocco, The Gambia and Upper Volta as president of Save the Children Fund. She was making an official tour of India when Mrs Gandhi was assassinated.

While attending an opera gala dinner in Los Angeles, Anne proved how much more relaxed she is now with the media by announcing wryly, 'I feel I am not supposed to appreciate anything that doesn't have four legs, barks or neighs.'

Princess Anne's three-day visit to Los Angeles that began on 8 July 1984 focused on British links with Hollywood and Britain's contribution to the Olympic Arts Festival. On a short tour of Hollywood, Anne met actress Joan Collins (far left), Elizabeth Taylor, Stewart Grainger, and other British-born stars at the première of Scottish director Bill Forsyth's film *Comfort and Joy*. Determined to see the less elegant side of the city, Princess Anne visited Para Los Niños, a converted warehouse home for abused children, where she met an eight-year-old girl who had twice been raped by her sister's boyfriend and the six-week-old child of a teenage heroin addict. She sat in on a lesson at the slum centre and watched a demonstration of break-dancing (left). The leader said afterwards, 'I didn't know who she was, but she was a real nice lady.' Later in July, Princess Anne and Captain Mark Phillips attended a Berkeley Square Ball – one of London's most prestigious charity events. Princess Anne (left, bottom) wore a blue and green silk dress and Captain Phillips sported a red carnation in his buttonhole. The Princess is patron of the Ball that in 1984 raised money for MENCAP, the NSPCC, the Princess's Charitable Trust and the Royal Jubilee Trust

THE QUEEN MOTHER

In the year of her 84th birthday, Queen Elizabeth the Queen Mother fulfilled a characteristically busy schedule, winning new admirers and consolidating her unrivalled reputation for good-natured warmth and charm. For this most regal of ladies, the highlights of the year were undoubtedly the birth of her fourth great-grandchild, Prince Henry, and the ceremonies recalling the Allied invasion of Normandy in 1944, which opened the way for the ending of a war that had deeply involved both her and her late husband, King George VI.

The birth of a second child to Charles, her favourite grandchild, gave the Queen Mother enormous pleasure. The baby arrived when she was enjoying her annual holiday in Scotland, which meant that although she was kept fully informed of the baby's progress by telephone, it was not until October that she saw young Harry for herself.

Back in June, at the height of a sun-filled summer, the Queen Mother attended two public functions at Portsmouth to commemorate the D-Day landings. She took part in a service of remembrance in Portsmouth Cathedral and unveiled a commemorative window, then went on to open the city's D-Day Museum at Southsea, admiring the exhibits and especially the detail in a large narrative embroidery depicting the Normandy landings and featuring the late King.

A keen racegoer, the Queen Mother was the focus of attention at Cheltenham in March (opposite); the following month her horse Special Cargo won the Whitbread Gold Cup at Sandown Park. Also in April the Queen Mother made a trip to Kent, stopping off at Lower Upnor to visit the Arethusa venture centre with its elaborate ship's figurehead (left). At Sandringham in July the Queen Mother enjoyed a walk along a wind-swept beach (inset left)

Despite her age the Queen Mother continues to enjoy robust health and maintains a lively interest in a wide variety of organisations and activities. She is colonel-in-chief of 18 British regiments, Warden of the Cinque Ports, and patron of some 300 bodies. She has been quoted as saying that 'work is the rent you pay for life' – and in her case the rent seems to be going up. The Queen Mother attended well over 100 public engagements in 1984 and assumed new responsibilities by becoming president of the Victoria Cross and George Cross Association, of which she is also patron.

April was a very special month for the Queen Mother in her role as racehorse owner – she celebrated the success of her horse Special Cargo in the Whitbread Gold Cup at Sandown Park.

There was another celebration during the year – for the Queen Mother's birthday. On Saturday 4 August, despite steady rain, a crowd of 500 gathered outside Clarence House to give their good wishes to the royal great-grandma. Shortly before 11 a.m. an elderly equerry came out of the gates and surveyed the crowd. The rain then stopped, and the strains of 'Happy Birthday to You' grew in crescendo as the band of the Second Battalion the Grenadier Guards marched past. The Queen Mother then made her appearance, wearing pale blue. She gave a gentle wave of her hand, inclined her head in that slightly shy manner and spoke a quietly repeated 'Thank you all.' She was answered by friendly cheers followed by the singing of 'For She's A Jolly Good Fellow'. Children darted forward to present her with cards and posies, which were gathered by a happy looking butler.

Just before 1 p.m. Prince Charles, Lady Sarah Armstrong-Jones and Viscount Linley arrived for lunch. The Queen Mother emerged again to welcome them and acknowledged further cheers before escorting her guests inside. As she did so the sun went in, too.

Students at Bedford College, University of London, provided plenty for the Queen Mother to smile about during a reception in May – and she, in puckish mood, also prompted many a chuckle (top). In February at a community centre in Swiss Cottage, north London, she obviously enjoyed her meeting with an African dressed in tribal costume (above). In July, at a Wolfson Home in Tottenham, north London, the Queen Mother chatted to senior citizens and admired a fabric collage specially created to mark the event (right)

The Queen Mother has a special knack of getting on well with young people. While visiting Stockwell Junior School in south London in July she watched the school band play – then asked if she could have a go on the maracas. Simon Lewis, 11, handed them over (inset, right) and the Queen Mother tried them out (right), shaking them in time to 'Island in the Sun'. Said Simon: 'Man, that lady . . . she sure got rhythm. She can play with us anytime'

PRINCESS MARGARET

For much of her life Princess Margaret has lived in the shadow of her elder sister, the Queen, and at the centre of controversy. She has never made a secret of the fact that she prefers the Bohemian company of artists and dancers to the sometimes restrictive rigours of formal royal life. Likewise, she has never been allowed to forget the contrast between the Queen and herself; whereas her sister is health-conscious, does not smoke or drink and enjoys modest forms of relaxation, Margaret has always been portrayed as a woman who has been dogged by illness, likes a cigarette and a whisky and soda and indulges herself on the exotic beaches of the Caribbean island of Mustique. Following her relationship with Roddy Llewellyn she was at a very low ebb – the Queen had expressed her disapproval, and Margaret was overweight and out of favour with the public.

Now, at the age of 54, she has slimmed down considerably, her blue eyes have regained their sparkle and she has done much to consolidate her role as a thoroughly professional, if still slightly reluctant, member of the royal family. Although no lover of small-talk, the Princess performs her wide variety of engagements conscientiously and

At a charity reception in London in April Princess Margaret (far left) handed over the keys of a new minibus to be used to transport underprivileged young people – this was just one of her many engagements for children's associations. In August the Princess, in her capacity as president of the NSPCC, attended a charity performance of the hit musical, *42nd Street* (left). The previous month, as a proud mother, she had opened Viscount Linley's new furniture crafts workshop in Betchworth, Surrey, using an outsize saw to cut the ribbon (top)

is particularly popular at fund-raising events where her presence is sure to boost attendance. For her part, Margaret shows great interest in her responsibilities towards children, and continues to be an active president of both the National Society for Prevention of Cruelty to Children and its Scottish counterpart. And, of course, she enjoys any function connected with the arts. Among many others during 1984, she attended the Sony radio awards ceremony at the Hilton hotel in London, opened a permanent public exhibition of Court Dress and Victorian Rooms at Kensington Palace and was guest of honour at the first night of the musical *42nd Street* at the Drury Lane Theatre, London.

However, it is the Princess's patronage of the Royal Ballet that gives her the greatest pleasure, for it is here that she finds people with whom she feels most at home, and who appreciate her for the witty, cultured and fun-loving person that she is.

In June the Princess paid a two-day visit to Ulster. Amid tight security she attended engagements to mark the centenary of the NSPCC and presented the 1984 Queen's Award for Export Achievement. And as president of the Girl Guides Association she delighted thousands of children on a mass rally at the Northern Ireland Guides Training Centre (left). Later in the month Margaret created a royal precedent when she played herself in an episode of *The Archers* (top, with Sara Coward and Arnold Peters)

THE DUKE & DUCHESS OF KENT

During the year Edward, Duke of Kent, and the Duchess of Kent followed a crowded schedule based on their special areas of interest.

The duke's diary contained many engagements connected with his position as vice-chairman of the British Overseas Trade Board. Twice in 1984 he made overseas visits to promote the interests of the board. In May he visited Morocco, and two months later travelled to New York and the American Midwest, meeting marketing executives and fronting the United Kingdom's efforts to increase the sales of British products to foreign buyers; the presence of a royal duke adds a touch of glamour to what is essentially a practical sales drive.

Sports bodies also claim much of the duke's time. He is president of both the Football Association and the All England Lawn Tennis and

Before embarking on a strenuous round of spring and summer engagements the duke and duchess enjoyed a brief holiday in Mustique shortly after the duchess's 51st birthday on 22 February. A week or two after their return (above) the duchess took the salute at the annual Sovereign's Parade at the Royal Military Academy, Sandhurst, held on 6 April (right, inspecting the cadets). In May, as a member of the Not Forgotten Association, the duchess went to Buckingham Palace (left) to meet former servicemen at a dedication ceremony for a new bus bought for the transport of disabled war veterans

Croquet Club. At Wimbledon in May he unveiled the Fred Perry gates and statue, and in June and July he and the duchess attended the tournament itself on several days, and the duchess presented the winners' trophies after the finals.

As president of the Royal Agricultural Society the Duke of Kent paid a two-day visit to the Royal Show at Stoneleigh, Warwickshire, in early July. A month earlier, on 6 June, he had taken the salute at the Beating Retreat by the massed bands of the Household Division on Horse Guards Parade.

The Duchess of Kent also has many commitments of her own. On 27 March she made the presentation at the annual Composer's Award reception in London, and on 23 May, as patron of the Yehudi Menuhin School, she hosted the school's 21st anniversary concert in the State apartments of St James's Palace. The Duchess of Kent is also president of the Royal Northern College of Music and attended college functions in Manchester on 28 and 29 June. In September, as patron, she was in the audience for the finals of the world-famous Leeds International Piano Competition. Earlier in the year, on 12 May, she had attended the Leeds University Open Day in her capacity as Chancellor of the University.

The Duchess of Kent is also controller commandant of the Women's Royal Army Corps and colonel-in-chief of the 4th/7th Royal Dragoon Guards, and in these roles visited British units in West Germany on 16 and 17 May. She also took the salute at the Sovereign's Parade at Sandhurst in April.

The Duchess of Kent listens intently to the speech given by the Emir of Bahrain at a banquet held in London during his State visit in April (left). The Duke of Kent took part in the clay pigeon shoot for royalty and celebrities held in Wales in July in aid of the Save the Children Fund (inset, far left). An enthusiastic sportsman, the duke was a member of the winning team

This official photograph of the Duke and Duchess of Gloucester was taken to mark the couple's 12th wedding anniversary on 8 July 1984

THE DUKE & DUCHESS OF GLOUCESTER

Just as his uncle, George VI, did not expect to be King, so Richard, Duke of Gloucester, did not expect to inherit the title; his elder brother William was killed while piloting a plane in an air race on 28 August 1972. The son of Prince Henry (third son of George V) and Alice (daughter of the seventh Duke of Buccleuch), Richard was born in 1944. A shy, quiet man, he had hoped to pursue his career as an architect in relative obscurity, living with his Danish wife Birgitte (*née* Van Deurs) in a converted warehouse in Dockland, but his father's death in 1974 gave him the dukedom with all its attendant responsibilities.

Among other things, the duke is Grand Prior, St John Ambulance Association, patron of ASH (Action on Smoking and Health) and colonel-in-chief of the Royal Pioneer Corps. The duchess is patron of the Asthma Research Council, colonel-in-chief of the Royal Army Educational Corps and commandant-in-chief, St John Ambulance in Wales. The duke and duchess carry out their numerous duties in modest style – he often surprises his hosts by turning up for engagements on a motorbike and she orders only five new outfits a year. They have two daughters – Davina and Rose – and a son, Alexander.

In May 1984 the Duchess of Gloucester attended the Pakistani Women's Group Spring Festival at the Intercontinental Hotel in Park Lane and was presented with a golden garland to wear (top left). On 13 June the duke and duchess attended a banquet at Hampton Court Palace (left) to commemorate the order of St John that helps to maintain the St John Ambulance Service

Failing health has recently caused
Princess Alice, Dowager Duchess of
Gloucester, to restrict the number of
public engagements she accepts. She has
led a full and interesting life, as is made
clear in her memoirs, which were
published in 1983

PRINCESS ALICE

PRINCESS ALEXANDRA

Beautiful, friendly and unpretentious, Princess Alexandra of Kent, cousin of the Queen, is an elegant, hardworking and very popular member of the royal team

orn on Christmas Day 1936, a fortnight after the abdication of her uncle Edward VIII, Princess Alexandra was, according to Queen Mary, 'the only nice thing to have happened this year'. The second child of the Duke and Duchess of Kent, Alexandra is sister to Edward (the present Duke of Kent) and Prince Michael of Kent. Her mother, Princess Marina, was the daughter of Prince Nicholas of Greece and her father, Prince George, the fourth son of George V, was tragically killed in a plane crash in 1942.

Alexandra was a bright, mischievous child, and the first British Princess to be educated at school with other children. She went to Heathfield near Ascot and is reputed once to have thrown a bucket of water over the matron's head.

When she was 15, Alexandra was taken away from school to prepare for her new role in public life following the Coronation of her cousin, Elizabeth. At first she found it difficult to behave with sufficient royal reserve but she emerged from a spell at a finishing school in Paris with poise and elegance. Her first solo tour – to Australia in 1959 – was a great success. She endeared herself to the Australians when she climbed into the back of the governor's limousine and sat on his new silk top hat. She held it up to the crowd and shouted, 'Look what I've done now!' Despite such blunders, her hard work and popularity were rewarded by the Queen who made her a member of the Royal Victorian Order.

Alexandra married Angus Ogilvy, the second son of the 12th Earl of Airlie, in Westminster Abbey on 24 April 1963. Her husband did not take a title and, with his easy-going charm and unpretentiousness, he soon became as popular as his wife. The couple moved to Thatched House Lodge in Richmond Park from where Princess Alexandra carries out her public engagements while her husband pursues his business career. They have two children, James and Marina.

Princess Alexandra has a hectic schedule of official engagements. She is patron of the National Association for Mental Health (MIND), patron of the English National Opera, Chancellor of Lancaster University and president of the World Wildlife Fund (UK). In March she attended the film première of *Yentl*, starring Barbra Streisand (who also co-wrote and produced it) in aid of MIND at the Leicester Square Theatre (above). In June she went to the USA accompanied by her husband to attend gala performances by the English National Opera in New Orleans (far left). Among many other engagements, the Princess also attended one of the three annual garden parties at Buckingham Palace (left) when the Queen and other members of the royal family meet those the Queen wishes to reward for public service or for outstanding services to the community

PRINCE AND PRINCESS MICHAEL OF KENT

In the past few years Prince and Princess Michael of Kent have emerged as one of the most popular of all royal couples. They receive no income from the Civil List – on marrying a Catholic and a divorcee, Prince Michael was forced to renounce his right to succession – and consequently they have to finance all their attendances at royal engagements themselves.

Given the limitation on their time and resources both the Prince and Princess undertake a considerable number of official engagements, many related to their own areas of interest and concern. During 1984 Prince Michael, a keen motorist, visited the British Motor Industry's Heritage Trust at Strudley, Warwickshire, attended several functions as president of the Institute of Motor Industries, watched the British Grand Prix in July as president of the Royal Automobile Club and, in the same month, started the Round Britain Offshore Powerboat Race at Portsmouth.

Princess Michael is passionately involved in her work as a Trustee of the Victoria and Albert Museum in London and in May was guest of honour at the important Bankers' Trust Concert and Dinner. The glamorous Princess is also much in demand as a media celebrity guest. In January, she was the castaway on Roy Plomley's BBC radio's *Desert Island Discs*, and in May she was a guest on Maria Aitken's television chat show, *Private Lives*.

Since marrying in 1978, Prince Michael (far left, top) has left the Army and now works in the city as director of two companies. His wife, Marie-Christine, largely has her time taken up with running the family home of Nether Lypiatt Manor in Gloucestershire. Although they receive no money from the Civil List, the couple undertake a full round of engagements. Prince Michael attends functions as president of the Royal Patriotic Fund and patron of the Museum of Army Flying, among others, and is an increasingly popular figure (above left, at the Windsor Horse Show). The stylish Princess is equally busy. As a Trustee of the Victoria and Albert Museum, with which she is greatly involved, she attended their G.P. & J. Baker Centenary Exhibition in May (above). Known as a vivacious and crowd-pulling guest, she is much in demand. Early in the year she opened *A Celebration of English Gardens* at Claremont Gardens, Esher (far left) and made a preview visit to the Spring Fair at the Kensington and Chelsea Town Hall (left)

THE YOUNGER GENERATION

Having been brought up in a much more relaxed atmosphere than their parents, today's royal children are willing – and able – to make their own way in a highly competitive world with a wide variety of skills and accomplishments.

Three-year-old Zara Phillips (below, with the Queen) and her brother Peter (right, bottom, with his mother, father and the Earl of St Andrews at Windsor) are both kept out of the limelight as much as possible. Peter, a confident and unspoilt seven-year-old, is due to start at a co-ed preparatory school in Dorset in 1985. Both Princess Margaret's children are involved in the arts. Lady Sarah Armstrong-Jones (top right) spent six months in the film business, and then in September 1984 started a two-year course in fabric design. Viscount Linley (far right) is now established as a furniture craftsman

Lady Helen Windsor, aged 20 (below, with her mother, the Duchess of Kent, and ex-King Constantine of Greece at Wimbledon), has already established her independence. Living in a flat in Knightsbridge, she worked for some time as a receptionist in an art gallery, later taking a course in French at the *Institut Français*. In September 1984 she started her 'first serious job' at Christies, the auctioneers. Marina Ogilvy (right), daughter of Princess Alexandra, has largely kept out of the public eye. At age 18, she is an accomplished pianist and a keen dancer

INDEX